BEYOND MY FATHER'S FARM

BEYOND MY FATHER'S FARM

An Autobiography

GEORGE J. ZELLER

ISBN 0-7414-5157-3

To order online, visit: www.bbotw.com

Additional copies of this book also may be ordered through your local bookstore.

Published by:

INFI∞ITY
PUBLISHING.COM

1094 New DeHaven Street, Suite 100
West Conshohocken, PA 19428-2713
Info@buybooksontheweb.com
www.buybooksontheweb.com
Toll-free (877) BUY BOOK
Local Phone (610) 941-9999
Fax (610) 941-9959

Printed in the United States of America

Printed on Recycled Paper

Published February 2009

To my beloved Katie,

For your loving ways…

And your devotion to the three of us.

CONTENTS

Part IV   CHANGING TIMES

DEDICATION

I dedicate this book to the memory of my parents, Walter Cecil Zeller and Otillia Schmitt Zeller, and to my memories of my wonderful in-laws, Fred and Olga Buechel, but specifically to my wife, Katherine (Katie) and our children John and Katherine.

I also dedicate this book to my older brother and sister, Walter and Mary Ann, who unknowingly inspired me to write this book.

ACKNOWLEDGMENTS

To my wife Katie a very special thanks, for her never-ending support and encouragement. Katie was my proofreader of at least a hundred times; she tirelessly read my memoirs, found my mistakes, corrected my grammar, and offered many helpful suggestions.

A very special thank you to John Knowles Probst, a talented retired college professor and a successful author. He helped me, a total stranger; he read and critiqued my manuscript not once but twice, offering solid suggestions, and directions to improve the content and layout of my memoirs, and gave me encouragement. I would have loved to have been a college student in John Knowles Probst's classroom; he has such a unique talent, a special gift of communicating his knowledge; he opened my eyes so I could see and understand. www.johnknowlesprobst.com

Many thanks to Emily Worthy Carmain, the owner of Noteworthy Editing on Amelia Island, Florida, for her excellent editing and smoothing skills, suggestions, and her pleasant, helpful, and professional way.

A special thanks to all who helped me with my story and gave me encouragement along the way.

Prologue

The torrential rain pounded against my window, and then loud cracks of thunder followed by brilliant bolts of lighting brought my dreams to a sudden halt and threw me into a state of wakefulness. Where on earth was I?

I opened my eyes and looked around in fear; nothing looked familiar. The seven-by-twelve-foot room was furnished with military-style cot, small dresser, desk and chair, and there was a very small closet; no shades or curtains on the window. After I shook the cobwebs away, I exhaled in relief, recognizing the room I had rented at the Rochester YMCA for seven dollars a week.

Now I knew where I was: I was free! I had left the farm just yesterday and come, at the tender age of seventeen, to make my way in the world, as far as my limited means and brief life experience would allow me. I had escaped from the oppression of my father's smoldering wrath.

The room was small, but perfect, by my standards. As I gazed out the seventh-floor window, watching the rain beat against the glass panes, I thought that this was probably one of the last October rains giving the trees a final drink before they went to sleep for the winter.

Then I realized it was six-thirty Sunday morning. What would I do today? Explore, perhaps! My excitement rose.

Then my thoughts flashed back to Ma, the hate I held in my heart for Pa and the painful past of our family. I took a deep breath and tried to recall some of my loving memories about the farm...

CHAPTER I

Early Years

Walter, Mary Ann and I are the offspring of Til and Cec Zeller. Our mother, Otillia "Til" Schmitt Zeller, was of the Catholic faith. Our father, Walter Cecil Zeller—nicknamed "Cec"—was Protestant.

Pa was born in 1903, the oldest boy in a family of eight children, seven of whom survived. He grew up in Rochester, New York, where he completed the eighth grade in Public School #36.

His father worked in a shoe factory. For a short while, the family lived in Short Tract, New York, in a small farming community where Pa's father and mother operated a farm. But not long afterward, his father returned with his family to Rochester and the shoe factory.

Ma, born in 1901, was a middle child in the Schmitt family of five boys and three girls. She grew up in the Schmitt Grocery Store, where the family also conducted the business of horseradish processing and bottling, growing and selling flowers and real estate. From their holdings, one could assume the Schmitts were financially well off. Yet Ma's education, like my father's, stopped at the eighth grade.

....

They were married in June 1929 in Rochester—four months before the stock market crash that launched the Great Depression.

Their first child, Walter, was born at home in April 1930. On Christmas Eve in 1931 a stillborn daughter, Carol, was born. The next child, Mary Ann, arrived in May 1935.

I was the youngest, coming along in July 1938. I was baptized George J. Zeller, for my uncle, George John Schmitt, a kind family man who raised zinnias, asters, chrysanthemums and a hundred thousand gladiolas, in addition to working his janitor job in an apartment complex.

....

For some time during the Depression years Ma and Pa lived in the Schmitts' rental property, and the Schmitts gave work to Pa. Ma and Pa purchased and charged most of their food at Schmitt's Grocery Store.

I remember, as a boy, hearing Ma say that during the Depression Grandma Schmitt gave credit to many families that did not have money to purchase groceries. She emphasized how much these people appreciated Grandma Schmitt's kindness, and most never forgot it. Some were not able to pay their bills until many years later, and there were quite a few who never paid their grocery bill with the Schmitts.

According to Ma, Grandma explained that their debtors just needed the money for something else, and probably needed it more than she did. Ma told me that she and Pa finally paid off their grocery bill to Schmitt's Grocery Store shortly before Grandma Schmitt died in 1947.

Years ago, I was told that my Grandpa Schmitt died as a result of injuries he received when he fell from a horseradish wagon, but I also heard that my grandfather died of gunshot wounds inflicted by someone from the Wegman Brothers' Grocery, the family's fierce business competitors located just down the street. That bit of intelligence, however, was never completely explained and has remained one of the family's "hushed-up" legends.

....

According to the comments of family members, Pa must have swallowed his pride often during his first ten years of marriage. During our country's hard times in the 1930s, Pa also worked for a while as a laborer six days a week in the Burkhart greenhouses. His pay included a house and a dollar a day in cash and all the fresh vegetables his family could use. Ma told me stories about that time in their lives. They were generally broke but were very happy then.

Sometime around 1939 or 1940, our family moved to a rental house in the outskirts of Rochester. Directly across the street was the large home of Greece's town Supervisor, Gordon Howe. In 1939, Pa's brother Clifford helped him get a higher paying job at Carborundum Manufacturing Company in Buffalo. However, because of the sizeable distance away from our home, Pa stayed with Clifford and his wife, Vera, and came home to his own family only on weekends.

World War II came, and Pa found work back in Rochester at Delco and also worked part-time at the Boxard Company on the Genesee River. About 1941 the family moved about five miles to a nice apartment above the A&P Grocery Store in Charlotte, on the outskirts of Rochester. Ma worked part time cleaning houses for wealthy people.

It was a short walk to Charlotte Beach on Lake Ontario and to Holy Cross Catholic Church. Walter went to Holy Cross Grammar School in the seventh and eighth grades and then to Aquinas Catholic High School for his freshman and part of his sophomore year. Mary Ann and I attended Holy Cross School.

Walter was an Altar Boy at Holy Cross. He had several paper routes, delivering the papers on his big green bicycle with skinny tires. On Sundays, Ma bought a one-dollar bus pass, providing transportation anywhere the bus went in Rochester for the next week. It was a very happy time, as I recall.

At Charlotte Beach we went swimming, ate frozen custard at Abbot's Custard Stand, rode on the merry-go-round, and enjoyed band concerts in the park. We met the Brickler family, who lived down the street, and our families were good friends for many years.

CHAPTER II

Pa's Dream Farm

Shortly after World War II ended in 1945, Pa bought his dream farm. The forty-eight-acre farm, commonly known as the "old Beachum farm," had not been worked since 1934. It was located on the outskirts of Mumford, New York, a town of some two hundred people, situated about twenty-five miles southwest of Rochester.

One yellow flashing light on Route 383 marked the center of Mumford's business district, and Baldeck's Grocery & General Merchandise, Sheedan's Grocery, McDonald's Tavern, Frey's Hardware Store, a Post Office, Sam's barbershop, and Whiteside's two-pump gas station provided for the basic needs of the town folks.

Pa bought the last house on Armstrong Road that had running water, located about one mile east of town. Armstrong Road was at the top of a hill that ran parallel to Oatka Creek, approximately a third of a mile away.

In November 1945, our family moved to the farm. Like all children, the first things I remember from those early times were about the house we lived in.

The house at 567 Armstrong Road was probably a hundred and twenty-five years old. Its cellar walls were built of stone, and the floor beam supports were logs, many with their bark still in place. The cellar was divided into three sections; each of the rooms was of stone construction built in self-contained sections and connected by doorways. The cellar included a cistern and a root cellar with a dirt floor.

The three-story, uninsulated clapboard house contained a kitchen, dining room, living room, and five bedrooms, two on the second floor, two off the living room, and Ma and Pa's bedroom, located off the dining room, at the rear of the house. In the hallway on the second floor, an attic was accessible by using a ten-foot ladder through a trap door in the ceiling. The natural gas pipes once used for lighting the house were still in place.

The kitchen had a large walk-in pantry, where dishes, pots, pans and food were stored on shelves, as the kitchen had no cupboards. The sink's one spigot provided cold drinking water from the town of Mumford; a hand pump supplied water from the cistern. The kitchen sink drain was through a pipe out of the back of the house onto the ground, an open leach field area.

The house had no central heat or plumbing, but there was a potbelly stove in the living room that could be fired up when company came or when the weather was extremely cold. Over the years, the house apparently had been added to in three separate stages, as the floors were uneven between the kitchen and the dining room as well as between the dining room and the living room.

A three-hole outhouse, located some distance beyond the side porch, was reached by going down a flight of eight concrete steps, followed by twenty or so steps across the grass. Nearby there was a plum tree, the smoke house and a wood shed that sometimes were well shaded by a large maple tree.

About seventy feet away from the wood shed was a corn crib, and adjacent to it was a two-story building used as a chicken coop.

Beyond that stood a huge, two-story red barn with a gambrel roof, a silo, and a milk house. The cows, horses, and baby pigs were housed in the lower level of the barn; hay, straw and grain were stored on the main floor. My father or brother often milked the cows by the light of a kerosene lantern. The wood beams in the barn were enormous, with the peak of the gambrel roof approaching fifty-five feet. The main floor was constructed of three separate layers of flooring, and the top layer was hardwood, as smooth as a dance floor. On that floor Walter put up a large backboard and basket for playing basketball.

Two large maple trees stood by our house in the front yard, near the road. The pigpen was beyond the large fenced barnyard. Nearby there were four apple trees, each a different variety, and two pear trees. Approximately six hundred feet behind the house, the Baltimore & Ohio railroad tracks sliced our farm in two.

. . . .

Our family had left behind in Rochester the comforts of indoor plumbing, running hot water and central hot-water heating to move to this primitive, run-down farm. Ma hated the move to the farm and its kitchen range that burned wood or coal on one side and natural gas on the other. She hated the top-loading icebox on the back porch.

She hated her loss of freedom. She was no longer able to take the city bus to visit her aging, sick mother and her family or go shopping at the big department stores or attend daily Mass at Holy Cross Church. The St. Patrick's Catholic Church in Mumford was a satellite church, where services consisted of one Mass on Sunday and one Mass at six a.m. on Holy Days of Obligation, and confessions were heard once a month. The main church, St. Columba Catholic Church, was located two and a half miles away in Caledonia. To make matters worse, Ma did not drive.

The purchase of the farm was Pa's dream, not a shared dream. I've always wondered whether Pa gave any consideration at all to Ma's feelings. And yet she handed over her savings that she had earned from cleaning houses to be used toward the down payment on the farm, money she had been saving for a long time to buy a special winter coat.

My father was a domineering individual who towered over the other household members—not in height, for he was only about five feet four inches tall, but in voice and harsh disciplinary manner. At forty-two years old, he had a stocky, strong build and weighed about one hundred sixty-five pounds. He wore bifocal glasses with small gold colored rims, had brown eyes, and was bald with a little brownish gray hair around the rim of his head. He usually was dressed in dark blue laborer clothes, and his hands, the hands of a laborer, were rough to the touch.

By nature he had a very cold personality; he was a quiet man, an insensitive, stern man, severely critical of everything I said and did. This demanding individual with his bifocals seemed to look right through me. And when he spoke, I could only compare his voice to that of Frank Morgan, the Wizard of Emerald City in "The Wizard of Oz," just before the Wizard was exposed as a fraud by Dorothy's dog Toto. I always felt like the cowardly lion or the tin man, and I think my brother did also.

"When I say something, THAT'S WHAT I MEAN!" I remember he would shout, "Walter, you don't wait 'til tomorrow to do it, YOU DO IT NOW! NOT ONE MINUTE LATER, NOW! JUST AS I TOLD YA!" He would yell at Walter or me in a thundering voice. We in turn trembled and would never think of questioning his ever-demanding authority.

All the hair on the back of my neck would rise at just hearing his footsteps as he entered the house. In time I would come to find that if he wanted something from you he could be warm and charming, but once he got his way, you were again ignored.

If opposites attract, that was certainly true in my parents' marriage. Ma by her very nature was friendly, likeable, easy to talk to and always a friend even to strangers in need. She possessed a strongly positive attitude, and in so many ways that my father was not, she was a loving parent. If Pa was the towering Wizard of Oz, Ma was certainly the Good Witch of the North, Glinda.

Usually wearing a housedress and a full apron, she cleaned the house and cooked like other wives and mothers in the 1940s. For relaxation, she loved nature and walking in the cedar woods. Sitting on a log by Oatka Creek, she would quietly enjoy the serenity of the tranquil moving water and the surrounding woods.

In later years terrible depths of depression would replace Ma's quiet, unassuming attitude. But that was far ahead.

While walking in the back fields with my mother we would gather wild flowers, sometimes violets; she would put them in a vase and decorate the house. A special bouquet was always placed before her statue of the Sacred Heart of Jesus, for which she had a special devotion.

At forty-four, Ma had a warm beautiful smile and her blue eyes sparkled as she spoke. She was about five feet two inches tall and weighed about one hundred thirty pounds, perhaps slightly stocky, and she had curly, fine, dark brown hair and fair, soft skin.

Ma's bright, genuine smile went with a caring, warm-hearted personality. She was smart and was not afraid to help anyone having a problem. Her voice was always gentle as she spoke the truth, and she had a disposition that saw the good in everyone.

On occasion she loved to dress up and go dancing with Pa at the Top Hat Grill. Often as she cooked she hummed softly or sometimes sang "Somewhere Over the Rainbow." Most every week she would bake several delicious apple pies with a flaky crust that would melt in your mouth. She loved flowers and enjoyed working in the garden. There was no denying her congenial personality, a carbon copy of that seen in all of her warm, loving Schmitt family.

············

Walter was fifteen years old that November when he entered Caledonia High School in his sophomore year. The high school was approximately two miles from home with no school bus available.

Mary Ann was ten years old and in the sixth grade, and I, at seven, was in the third grade, when we enrolled at Mumford Union School that fall. My class had seven pupils, all the way from the third through the seventh grade. The three-room red brick schoolhouse had a bell tower and a large playground with swings, slides, and a teeter-totter.

············

The first neighbors we met were Hattie and Louis (Louie) Johnson, a black couple who lived kitty-corner across the road. They had no well, and each day Hattie came to fetch a bucket of drinking water from the spigot in our kitchen. The Johnsons had a cistern that provided rainwater for their other requirements.

The Johnsons were friendly people, and our families quickly became good friends. Hattie was about forty years old, about five feet tall and slightly built; she was a happy person. She told us that Louie had been a professional boxer, but before she would agree to marry him, he had to give up boxing for good. Louie, a couple of years older than Hattie, was a big, strong man, about six-foot-two, with a winning smile and a laugh bigger than life. He was as gentle as he was big and had a beautiful voice when he sang.

They had no children, and it was obvious that they made up for the loss through their kindness to the kids in the neighborhood. Louie taught Mary Ann and me how to jump rope together using a long section of clothesline; sometimes he even joined in. By himself Louie used a piece of one-and-a-half-inch hemp rope; he could jump a hundred and fifty times with ease, using a variety of patterns and speeds.

Louie was a self-employed contractor; he delivered coal, sand and gravel to the people in the surrounding towns. Sometimes, on Saturdays, he would take me with him to make deliveries in his old dump truck. I was thrilled to be with my friend Louie. Most times, he would stop and buy me an ice cream cone at Sheehan's Grocery on our way home.

Then, in the spring of 1948, the Johnsons' landlord put the property up for sale and the Johnsons moved seven miles away to the hamlet of Garbutt. The two families kept in touch for a while, but eventually we lost touch with Hattie and Louie.

The Livermores bought the property and moved in with their three young children, Harold, about seven years old, Maureen, six, and Grant, four. Before moving into the house, Mr. Livermore installed running water. He came to the house on weekends to dig a ditch so the town of Mumford could run a water line from the road through the lower part of the cellar wall.

My siblings and I were somewhat older than the Livermores, but we all became good friends. Ma formed a strong friendship with Lorraine Livermore, and they shared many a recipe and home remedy. The Livermore family was making it on a shoestring; however, Mrs. Livermore was a kind, loving woman and frequently made sugar cookies for all the children in the neighborhood.

CHAPTER III

Difficult Days

Shortly after the move to Mumford, Pa got a job shoveling coal into the boilers at Ebsary Gypsum mine in nearby Wheatland. He worked the "C" shift, eleven-thirty p.m. to eight a.m. Pa came home from work and then worked on the farm before going to bed about three p.m., so when we came home from school we had to be quiet.

Growing up, Pa, the eldest boy of the seven children, had been well accepted by his family. As most young men do, he had big dreams; however, he had never learned a trade and had only an eighth-grade education. In the mid-1920s that background would probably have been enough to help him attain most reasonable goals. But with the arrival of the Great Depression, Pa's hopes and dreams, like everyone else's, were put on hold. From comments I heard, it seems that Pa had a hard time accepting the kindness and generosity extended by the Schmitt family, as he continued to dream of being his own boss and owning a farm.

However, when the economy improved, he considered only himself, only his dream, in purchasing the farm. He did not thoroughly investigate what the additional requirements would be—namely, how much it would cost to upgrade the house to provide indoor plumbing, including hot water and a tub, central heat, electricity in all the rooms, the conveniences that would make the home somewhat comparable to the one Ma had left.

If Pa had considered the cost of a used tractor and related basic equipment, two-blade plow, disc, drag, cultivator, manure spreader and a wagon, I am reasonably sure he would have realized that his chances of success were nil and he was doomed from the start. I believe that, after the farm was purchased, Pa realized he had no way out.

His frustration and fears of financial ruin and personal failure continued to grow. The times would not allow him to divorce his wife and abandon his children. His family and brothers and sisters would never accept him if that happened. To run away would have resulted in bankruptcy and disgrace to the Zeller name; this was not acceptable either.

So he lived with his fears and frustrations, which eventually consumed him, and shortly thereafter he began to vent his frustration on his wife and children, while trying to save face, as he saw it, with his four brothers and the Zeller family.

Pa made a bad decision in buying the farm, but he made a horrible mistake in treating his wife and children as though they were the cause of his problems, the reasons for him not being a very successful farmer. He always presented himself to himself as a success, and he lived this fallacy. Through it all, it appeared that in Pa's mind he did not have the acceptance of his brothers. In reality, while they laughed at him, they still loved and accepted him.

I believe Pa had a dream of a beautiful farm; but that was it—just a dream. He had not considered the facts or reached a positive agreement with his wife. He had no money or available credit to purchase equipment he needed, and he really had little awareness of the effort this was going to take. Pa just acted before he thought things out thoroughly. ·He wanted to show the Zeller family that he was a success; after all, he was the oldest son.

He clung to his brothers, where he had acceptance, rather than placing his wife and children first in his thoughts. When his family would come to visit, he would quickly go to McDonald's Tavern and buy a couple of quarts of beer for his parents and brothers. He always had time for them and money for beer for them, although he didn't buy any pop for us. He was always happy to see them and then he would brag about all of the things that he had accomplished.

Pa never acknowledged any of the help that he had received from his family. This scene was repeated over and over again and was very hurtful to our family; no one wants to feel used. I always wondered why he treated us this way. Why didn't he enjoy us, or have time for us, or like us, as he liked his parents and brothers? I always wondered why; they didn't help him, we did. In return, he treated us as his subjects and took his frustrations and fears out on us.

When I was a little boy, I feared my father for his meanness and therefore rejected him. While I loved him because he was my father, I did not like him; nor did I feel comfortable with him. I felt that Pa was not looking out for each member of our family's future. I felt he was obsessed with his dream and his own image with his brothers. When his dream became a financial albatross, frustration, anguish and worry gave him no easy way out.

Ma worked hard and struggled to help Pa with his dream. She accepted the farm as a way of life. She resented that her husband continued to cling to his birth family. Ma tried hard to please him and his family by cooking delicious meals for them and catering to them. On the other hand, when Ma and Pa visited Grandma Zeller, she would often say, "I didn't fuss today," and would serve cold cuts for sandwiches.

The Zeller family, no matter how hard she tried to please them, probably because she was of the Catholic faith, never accepted Ma. I'm sure that Pa was well aware how his family was treating Ma, but obviously he didn't care; he never spoke up on her behalf to demand that his parents treat his wife right.

Ma made sure we kids attended Mass on Sundays, observed the church Holy Days, went to Confession, received Communion on Sundays, fasted during Lent, and did not eat meat on Fridays. Religion was practiced in our home daily, and Novenas were observed. Pa did not go to church, but he never spoke against the fact that we children were raised in the Catholic faith.

My brother, Walter, at seventeen years old was about five feet three inches tall, weighed about one hundred thirty-five pounds, and had blue eyes and light brown hair. He caught the bulk of Pa's frustrations and fears and was Pa's personal drudge; there was no amount of work that was too great to be given to him. He worked with the team of horses, plowing, dragging, cultivating, spreading manure, and tending the livestock, as though he was a full-grown man.

There were no rewards for his labor from Pa, not even a kind word, no compliments, no "fine job" or "thanks" or "I appreciate your help" or "the field sure looks nice." Pa just gave Walter more work orders and more criticism. If Pa was sleeping, he had written Walter's work orders on a blackboard. The dogs were treated better than Walter was—at least he petted the dogs.

When Pa would talk with his parents and brothers, he always said something like, "Look at that field... I just finished dragging the field," or "Look at that cornfield; I just finished cultivating that cornfield three days ago and it's already grown another foot."

In truth Walter finished cultivating that field a week ago and Pa took all the credit; he never acknowledged all the work that Walter and his family provided.

Walter was an excellent baseball player in high school and also enjoyed playing basketball. He played on the Mumford town team. In 1948, Caledonia won the baseball division championship and went on to play a game in Briggs Stadium in Detroit, Michigan. Pa never went to see him play baseball, not in high school, not in semi-pro leagues, never.

When Walter graduated from Caledonia High School in June 1948, he immediately moved out of the house to Rochester, some twenty-five miles away. Prior to graduation he had gotten a job with Western Union Telegraph Co. delivering telegrams. In early 1949, he went to work at Eastman Kodak Company.

....

Shortly after Grandma Schmitt died in 1947, Ma received her inheritance from the sale of several properties; the homestead and its adjoining two lots were not sold. All of Ma's inheritance was spent on improvements to our home including central heat, indoor plumbing, hot water heater, refrigerator, gas range, white metal kitchen cabinets and blue linoleum in the kitchen, wallpaper, and paint throughout the house.

Ma's brother-in-law, Bill DuBois, updated the electricity. Most of his work was very good, but there were surprises. In order to use one of the bedroom outlets, the cellar light had to be turned on. Harley Brickler plastered all the ceilings and walls. He would bring his wife and about six of his fourteen children with him. We played all day and late in the afternoon we cooked hot dogs and had a wonderful time.

Our farmhouse in Mumford, about 1951.

Ma's brother, Uncle Leo, rebuilt the front porch. I remember Pa's being upset with Uncle Leo for letting me use a hand saw to cut a board. He was concerned that I would not cut the board perfectly straight. I recall that Pa took all of the credit for all the remodeling and upgrading of the house, when in fact, without Ma's inheritance, none of it would have been possible. It is true that Pa did the preparation and repairs of the wood and the painting inside and out, and varnished the floors, but that was the limit of his contribution, as he had no money for any additional improvements.

Ma's inheritance paid for all of the improvements. I remember Ma crying after each of the Zeller family visits, recalling how Pa had talked about all of the improvements that he had made to the house when he spoke to his brothers' and parents. Pa never acknowledged the fact that all the money came from Ma's inheritance from her family.

The barn and silo of our farm, about 1951

· · · · · · · · · · · ·

Ma was comfortable with the way the home improvements and amenities turned out. She was now proud of her home, and was even happy with country living and the farm life. She enjoyed her home, and its surroundings, and had grown to love the serenity and quiet of the country, the spaciousness of our lawn and farm, and the birds and wild life.

She often walked through the apple orchard and the fields to the far end of the farm beyond the cedar forest. Whenever she walked through the fields our two dogs were always close by—Rover, a beautiful collie/shepherd and Lucky, Rover's son, a collie/shepherd mongrel and a large protective dog.

· · · · · · · · · · · ·

The Mumford Union Grammar School was located on Dakin Street, off Main Street nearly at the top of Mumford's big hill, about one mile from our farm. At the bottom of the hill lay the center of town with its small business district.

Almost daily after school, weather permitting, the boys would race their bicycles down Dakin Street, turning on to Main Street and down Mumford hill, where they turned east onto State Street and headed toward home.

On a fall day in mid-September of 1947, we raced as usual. However, when my nine-year-old cousin, Jimmy McCombs, came out of Dakin Street on his bicycle, turning onto Main, he did not see a truck coming. The truck struck him, and he was killed instantly. The rest of the boys, however, were already on State Street and unaware that the accident had occurred. We did not find out about it until later that afternoon.

It seemed like forever before the blood washed off the street. Jimmy looked like a beautiful doll, sleeping in the casket. I was one week younger than Jimmy and served as pallbearer with other classmates. It was a very sad time, my first face-to-face experience with death, and it had a lasting effect.

············

In the fall of 1947, Ma and Pa took Barbara and Patsy Butler into the family as foster children. These children, nine and eleven years old, from the Catholic Charities in Rochester, had already been in numerous foster homes. Ma and Pa treated them as if they were their own, including the assignment of chores and homework. While at times we had some problems, for the most part we had some wonderful times together.

The most difficult times for Patsy and Barbara were family visits, which were to be on a scheduled, semi-monthly basis. Sometimes, however, it was as much as a month or six weeks between visits.

We had some great times sledding and tobogganing on Livermore's and Baker's hills in the winter and swimming in the old swimming hole in Oatka Creek and playing baseball in the summer.

In late 1949 Patsy and Barbara moved to their Grandmother Butler's home on Gregory Street in Rochester to live with her and their father. I kept in touch with them until Barbara was eighteen and engaged to be married; afterward, we lost touch.

....

Mary Ann worked hard on the farm, but she was different from Walter or me. With brown eyes and brown hair, she was pretty and petite—about five feet tall and weighing perhaps a hundred pounds soaking wet.

She was smart like Ma and took after Ma in nature. In the eighth grade, Mary Ann had earned the highest marks in the class. However, for some reason unknown to the family, she was not given the title of valedictorian or allowed to give the commencement speech.

Jim Guthrie, the School Board President, found out about it, and he would not allow her accomplishments to go unnoticed at the graduation commencement exercises. When Mary Ann's name was called to receive her diploma, Jim Guthrie announced that she had the highest marks in the class, cited them, and so honored Mary Ann. Oh, how she beamed when she got her diploma!

In 1950, Caledonia High School centralized, taking in the towns and hamlets of Mumford, Wheatland and Clifton, to become Caledonia Mumford Central School. In high school Mary Ann continued to earn high marks, upper 90s in Latin, algebra, geometry, trig, biology, chemistry, physics, English and history. She graduated in 1953.

She wanted to be a Registered Nurse, but Pa would not support her. Instead, she went to work in the office of Eastman Kodak and moved about six months later from our home to share an apartment with a girl she worked with in Rochester.

CHAPTER IV
Christmas Trees, Horses
and Hay Wagons

During the summer when Walter was about seventeen, about once or twice a week he would take Ma, Mary Ann and me in the horse-drawn wagon to the far back muck field behind the cedar forest to weed and hoe sweet corn, melons and potatoes. Each time, as we went about halfway through the ten-acre cedar forest, we would check on a particular cedar tree that seemed to be shaped perfectly for a Christmas tree. It was so beautiful! We decided that this year the tree would be big enough, just perfect for our Christmas tree.

We picked quite a lot of sweet corn that year, and the potatoes also provided a good harvest, but the raccoons, woodchucks, and deer ate most of the melons. In late fall, after all the crops were in and everything ready for winter, Walter began to load the wagon with manure and cart it to the field beyond the forest. He would spread the manure, one pitchfork at a time, on the fields in preparation for spring planting. This was a huge job, with approximately twenty-five acres of ground to cover prior to spring plowing.

The weather was now cold, with a couple of inches of snow on the ground, and a constant sharp northwest wind blowing, often with a trace of snow in the air. I kept reminding Walter about the family Christmas tree in the cedar forest, asking over and over again, "Walter when are we going to cut down the Christmas tree? It's getting close to Christmas."

He replied, "Quit bugging me, George. I'll get to it one of these days. It's still too early."

"Okay, Walter, but please do it soon."

I waited through the weeks in great anticipation. Then one very cold day near the twentieth of December, on the way back home from the far muck field beyond the cedar forest, Walter stopped and cut the perfectly shaped cedar tree and brought it home and stuck it in the snow next to our house. I jumped up and down and hollered with joy!

Two days before Christmas the tree was set in its stand, then taken into the house and set up in the living room to let it thaw out and dry off so Ma and Pa could decorate it on Christmas Eve. A fire had been lit in the potbelly stove in the living room so the living room would be nice and warm for the ritual trimming of the tree. The near-perfect shaped cedar tree looked beautiful in the stand in the corner, and everyone was excited about Christmas.

Once the tree began to thaw out, though, the entire family noticed a foul odor, and the odor got stronger by the minute. We all sniffed the tree, and there was no doubt about it—it smelled like manure!

Pa asked Walter, "How did you bring the tree home? I'll bet you brought it home in the manure wagon. How many times do I have to tell you, Walter, to think about what you're doing?"

Just as Pa suspected, Walter had put the tree into the wagon on his way back from spreading the manure in the muck field. The tree of course had to be discarded. Poor Walter!

We all walked back to the cedar forest to select another tree, and Walter pulled the toboggan, carrying the new tree home. Every Christmas thereafter, he was teased about the almost perfect Christmas tree. Everyone but Walter had a good laugh, but he never saw the humor in the story, not then, and not now, more than sixty years later.

············

One Saturday morning in late September, Pa, Walter and Ma were out in the field pulling white marrow bean plants with a horse-drawn bean puller. The bean puller would skip about every fifth or sixth plant, and those left behind had to be pulled by hand. The bean plants were then loaded onto the wagon and taken to the barn where they would be stored until the threshing machine folks would come and process the beans.

At this point I had been told I could not work in the fields anymore because of the dust; I had a serious asthmatic condition, and Doctor Hare forbade it. Consequently, I was to stay at home and do the dishes and housework. Mary Ann, who was about thirteen years old, had permission to go to Baker's farm and pick up potatoes. She would be paid ten cents a bushel.

Before Mary Ann left, about seven forty-five a.m., she instructed me, "George, you are to make chicken noodle soup with bread and butter for lunch and have it ready to serve at noon, and be sure to have the table set on time." Mary Ann showed me the kettle of chicken broth in the refrigerator and the noodles and then left for work.

I did the dishes and cleaned the kitchen and then played with the dogs. About eleven o'clock I set the kitchen table for lunch and took the chicken broth out of the refrigerator and put it on the stove. I brought it to a boil and then added the package of Mueller's wide noodles and carefully stirred it. I was proud that lunch was ready with five minutes to spare.

At noon everyone came into the kitchen, hungry and ready to eat. Ma served the soup, and they all sat down and started to eat. Then the comments began: "How come this soup is so thick? This soup is like glue."

Ma said, "George, how did you make the soup?"

"I took the kettle of chicken broth out of the refrigerator, brought it to a boil and added the noodles."

"Well, that explains it, George. You should have cooked the noodles separately and then rinsed them with hot water before adding them to the broth." The grumbling continued, so Ma said with a smile, "At least this lunch will stick to your ribs, so don't complain."

Everyone laughed but gave me an evil eye, as this was all there was to eat, soup that would stick to your ribs, and homemade bread and butter—or nothing.

•••••••••••

About eleven o'clock one Saturday morning, when I was about nine years old, Walter said, "George, I'm leaving now to play in the high school baseball game. At noon I want you to feed the horses grain and hay, and then take the horses one at a time into the barnyard for water; Pa will be home shortly after noon."

I followed Walter's instructions and fed and watered Jack and Duke. However, by three o'clock Pa had not come home from work, so I decided to take Duke, the chestnut colored horse with a white face, for a ride. To be able to reach up and take the harness off the horse, I had to lead him over to the barnyard gate and climb up from gate to horse. I unfastened the harness lock on the bottom of Duke's horse collar and climbed up on the barnyard gate to reach the top of the horse's harness and remove it.

Unfortunately, I had forgotten to undo the belly strap, and when the horse walked out of the harness, he became entangled in the lines and stepped on the leather belly strap and broke it, also tearing a four-foot piece off the reins. The harness was too big and heavy for me to pick up and put it on its rack in the barn, so I left the harness on the ground in the barnyard and went for a ride on Duke in the pasture adjoining the barnyard.

I was having a good time riding Duke and had for the time being completely forgotten about Pa, who would arrive home soon and see the broken harness lying on the ground in the barnyard. However, that lapse of memory was short lived as Pa arrived home just a bit later. I slowly rode Duke into the barnyard to greet Pa and try to explain what had happened.

Pa looked over the damage to the harness and told me to get off the horse and put him in his stall in the barn. When I finished, he asked me, "George, what instructions did Walter give you?"

"Walter said to feed and water the horses, and I did as I was told!"

"Were you told you could take the horse for a ride?"

I replied, "No, Pa, but it was three o'clock and...."

Pa was getting angrier by the minute as he looked over the damaged harness with broken lines and reins, realizing that he would be unable to continue to cultivate the corn that day. He reached down and picked up one of the broken leather reins and told me to bend over his knee. Then he proceeded to give me a thrashing I would long remember.

Memories of our team of work horses—Duke, the white-faced horse, and Jack, the black horse, pulled the wagon we often rode in.

• • • • • • • • • • •

It was haying season in late June, and Pa was using a few days of vacation to get the hay in. During the previous days, Walter, Mary Ann, Ma and Pa had cut, raked, and piled the clover and timothy hay in stacks in the nearby eight-acre field. The hay was ready to be taken by horse and wagon to the barn and put into the loft for storage for winter feed for the cows and horses.

When the family got up shortly after daybreak to begin their morning chores, they noticed a red sky, indicating a possible approaching storm. Pa was uneasy, worrying that it would rain and spoil the hay before they could get it into the barn. So he told Walter to get the horses harnessed while he was finishing up the morning chores. Immediately following the chores, they had a quick breakfast that Ma and Mary Ann had prepared.

Walter was the first to finish breakfast and went to the barn and got the horses and hooked them up to the wagon on the main floor of the barn. He had opened the large back door of the barn as well as the front doors to aid in ventilation and help eliminate the possibility of spontaneous combustion with any damp hay.

Within a couple of minutes the rest of the family were right behind him and we climbed up on the wagon with the hay forks and headed for the hay field. Once in the field, it was a simple matter of moving the wagon forward between the rows, where piles of hay were situated about every twenty-five feet. Pa instructed me to sit in the driver's seat and hold the reins, but not to do anything else, as Pa would lead the horses down the row as needed. I was to hold the reins as a precaution against their running away if they were spooked, perhaps by a snake.

Ma stayed on the wagon and kept the hay load balanced as Walter, Mary Ann and Pa hoisted the hay with the hayforks up to Ma on the wagon bed. In a short time the wagon was loaded and Pa, Mary Ann and Walter climbed up on the wagon with me. Pa drove the team back to the barn, with Ma sitting on top of the hay.

Everything was going fine except that the weather was seriously threatening. Driving the team home was no big deal, as the horses surely knew their way to the barn. As the weather threatened more, with a loud rumble of thunder followed by a bolt of lightning, the pace of the horses increased to a pretty good clip.

The horses seemed to be getting away from Pa as they headed up the driveway toward the barn, and Pa was pulling back on the reins hollering, "Whoa... whoa... whoa... whoa." He yelled louder with each whoa, but to no avail.

The horses charged into the barn, the back door of which was still open for ventilation. Beyond the back door was a twenty-five-foot drop into the barnyard, with the manure pile below. The horses abruptly stopped when they saw the wide-open space below and reared up, striking the air wildly with their front feet.

As soon as Pa regained his composure, he checked the rig and the harness and found that Walter had not hooked the reins from the harness ring to the bridle ring when he changed the horses' halters to their bridles. Through the whole process of going to the field, loading the wagon with hay and returning to the barn, there had never been a time when the horses had been under complete control; they just knew the routine.

I still recall Pa shouting at Walter, "Now what do you have to say for yourself? How many times do I have to tell you to check your work over? Somebody could have gotten seriously hurt. How many times, Walter—how many times do I have to tell you? You are not as smart as you think you are."

The storm passed over shortly without a drop of rain, and all the hay in the field was brought into the barn that day without further incident.

•••••••••••

We always had a large garden, and Ma canned the vegetables, always a hundred quarts of tomatoes as well as tomato juice, corn, beans, beets and peas. Ma would make and can chili sauce, corn relish, mince meat, and jellies and jams. August was the main month for canning.

My job was to bring the empty jars up from the cellar and do the first washing of the jars. Ma and Mary Ann would give them a final washing and sterilizing. We all helped in the preparation and the filling of the jars, and Ma always took care of putting them into and out of the boiling water. Later, we all helped in putting the canned vegetables away in the cellar.

....

When I was eight, going on nine years old, Walter was injured while doing his chores. He cut the forefinger of his left hand to the bone while using a hand fodder chopper to cut corn stalks into silage for the cows. Blood was everywhere! Ma took care of him.

I don't remember how many stitches were required, but I do remember that, after the bandages came off Walter's hand weeks later, Ma had him wash dishes in soapy water almost every night for weeks to keep his skin soft. Eventually there was hardly a scar to be seen.

Around this same time, our pregnant Guernsey cow, Bessie, had gotten herself entangled into barb wire, resulting in nasty cuts to her rear legs, milk bag and udders. We cleaned her cuts on her udders and applied Bag Baum twice daily; Bessie's calf was due to be born shortly. Unfortunately, Bessie gave birth to a stillborn calf. Since she had now freshened, she needed to be milked twice every day. Pa milked Bessie in the morning as he was then working on the three-thirty p.m. to midnight shift. Walter's badly injured finger would not allow him to milk the cow; now this was my chance to do my part in helping out.

Ma stayed and supervised me for several days while I washed Bessie's udders in preparation and learned to sit on the three-legged milking stool and hold the milk pail between my legs. Milking her one squirt at a time was not as easy as I thought it was going to be, and occasionally Bessie would swat me in the face or head with her tail or move her rear leg and kick the pail.

After I got the hang of it and developed a milking rhythm, it took me about an hour to drain Bessie of her milk, which filled a thirteen-quart stainless steel pail. Pa told me it was very important to strip her of all of her milk or she could get sick. I can remember, by the light of the kerosene lantern, squirting the milk toward the cats that would sit up on their hind legs and catch the stream of milk. Ma said we could not drink the milk for about ten days, but it was all right to feed the milk to the pigs.

Milking Bessie and related duties became my chores every night for quite a while, and I was proud of being able to help out and felt very grown up. After ten days, the milk was safe to drink, and we kept whole milk for our family needs in the icebox. We always had plenty of milk, cream, homemade butter, buttermilk, and eggs on hand for cooking and baking, and we enjoyed lots of eggnogs for a treat. On the enclosed back porch, the rest of the milk was poured into a milk separator. At least once a week, the dairyman would stop by and pick up the cream we had saved.

Now that I was growing up at almost nine years old, as part of my new chores it became my responsibility to keep the lantern globe clean, using a wadded up newspaper, and to fill the lantern weekly with kerosene. I never minded cleaning the lantern's globe because, when soot built up on the globe, the amount of light lessened considerably.

I was comfortable all alone downstairs in the barn milking Bessie, always aware of the presence of the horses, calves, pigs and other animals. When I left the security of the animals in the barn and walked outside and closed the squeaking barn door on its rolling tracks, my fear of the dark amplified, and my security blanket became the lantern. As I walked past the chicken building, I hurried in the dark of night toward our house about three hundred feet away.

············

In 1948 or 1949, Mary Ann and I were very excited when the Town of Mumford announced the organization of a youth program for the eight- to sixteen-year-olds, on Tuesday and Friday nights in the large town hall. In the town hall there was a good sized basketball court where square dances for adults were held on Saturday nights.

Our neighbor, Mr. Livermore, was the principal volunteer who supervised the program. We played games on the main floor of the town hall, and sometimes did the Virginia reel; but to me the game that was the most fun was musical chairs. On Friday nights they also offered half-hour dance lessons. Ma gave us each a quarter as she was very keen on us taking ballroom dancing lessons, and we learned to dance the waltz, foxtrot, and jitterbug.

The final function for the year was held in May. The youth group had a pot-luck supper, and Mary Ann made a large Wesson Oil Party Chiffon Cake with whipped cream frosting. The four-layer round cake must have been twelve inches tall, filled between the layers and entirely covered with homemade whipped cream topping piled high with a swirl design. I can still see Ma standing in the kitchen as Mary Ann put the finishing touches on the cake; she was so happy and proud of her daughter. Oh, the taste of that sweet whipped cream cake; it was so delicious!

About all I actually remember about the ingredients of the cake are Wesson oil and a large number of eggs and the whipped cream topping. Since we lived on the farm, it was no problem—we had all the eggs, milk, butter, and cream we would ever need for any recipe, any day of the week.

....

I was about ten years old when our dog Rover gave birth to a litter of eight or nine mixed-breed pups. It was quite the sight, when Rover chased anything—the pups would all chase right behind her, all of them barking. We kept one pup and named him Lucky. Our family had a hard time trying to give away all of these mixed breed puppies; I think it took nearly six months before they were all given away, and I think Pa took the last three pups to work to give them away. The next year Rover gave birth to a litter of five or six pups.

I was in the barn when Pa said, "George, about those new pups of Rover's—we can not keep the puppies to give them away this year as it was a big problem last year. We will have to get rid of them right away and I need your help, as I am busy with my chores in the barn."

I said, "Okay, Pa, what do you want me to do?"

"George, I want you to watch the wood shed door until Rover leaves her pups in the shed and goes outside. Wait a few minutes until Rover goes back by the orchard; then I want you to go into the wood shed and quickly put all of the pups in this burlap bag, tie the bag closed and leave the wood shed. Then I want you right away to take the bag with the pups in it down to the creek; be sure the dogs are not following you.

"When you get to the edge of the creek by the shallow water just past the swimming hole, set the burlap bag down and pick up four or five flat stones; then untie the string on the top of the bag, put the stones in the bottom of the bag with the pups and retie the bag and put several knots in it. Then take the bag downstream a little bit where the next bend in the creek is and the water is deep, and drop the bag in the creek; and come home right away—I will be waiting for you."

He asked, "George, do you understand what I have told you to do?"

"Yes, Pa, I can do that."

I did exactly what Pa told me to do; I came right home and went to the barn to tell Pa that I was home.

"Hi, Pa, I did what you told me to do; I put the stones in the bag with the pups and retied it and dropped the burlap bag in the creek in the deep water downstream from the swimming hole. The burlap bag sank very quick."

"Okay, George, remember, you're not to talk about this with no one—do you understand me, boy, no one?"

"Yes, Pa."

"And today, all day you stay away from Rover! Now I want you to mix a pail of ground grain with a half pail of cracked corn with your hands very thoroughly, and try not to get it all over you, like you did the last time."

"Okay, Pa."

I mixed the ground grain and the cracked corn, but the grain was almost powder and I got it all over me just like the last time and I smelled like the grain; it was even in my hair. When I came out of the barn, there was Rover; she was still looking for her pups. But Pa had just told me to stay away from her for today.

Initially, I had felt good about helping Pa and that I was able to follow Pa's instructions exactly as he said. But I thought about what I had done after I watched Rover searching all over for her pups; then I knew what I had done was wrong. I had murdered Rover's pups. I felt real bad for a long time, I knew it was wrong; but I didn't tell anyone what I had done and I never said anything about how I felt to Pa.

....

When I turned twelve years old, Ma said to me, "George, this is the year you must learn in detail about cooking, baking, cleaning, washing, ironing, and all that is necessary in running a household. We will have a lot of fun!"

I recall listening to Ma explain that one never knows who you will end up with in marriage, and it only makes good sense never to go hungry for lack of knowing how to cook a meal or how to take care of yourself. Consequently, throughout my twelfth year, Ma taught and supervised me in baking several different pies, cakes, kuchen, and cookies and homemade bread, and cooking at least seven complete meals—including vegetable beef soup with plate beef, a baked chicken dinner with all the trimmings, hamburger steak smothered in onions with mashed potatoes and gravy, goulash, and German potato salad.

Ma taught me to use a pressure cooker when I made Irish stew or pork chops with sauerkraut and caraway seed, and not to be afraid of it. Mary Ann remembers the astonished look on my face when I told her, "I am not afraid, and I am never going to be afraid of that monster pressure cooker!"

She said, "George, you looked wild as you described adjusting the gas stove when the pressure cooker's gauge showed nineteen pounds of pressure and climbing, far above the recommended fifteen pounds of pressure, and the needle going into the black 'caution' area; you looked like you expected a hand grenade to explode in your hands at any second."

Cooking and baking actually were a lot of fun, as I recall. However, using the old wringer washing machine, hanging the clothes on the line and doing the ironing was not much fun at all, and house cleaning was even worse. I often wondered if I would ever turn thirteen! Could that thirteenth birthday come if I didn't learn to do all these things?

My mother, Otillia Schmitt Zeller,
August 1901—May 1967

CHAPTER V

Wonderful Times with the Schmitt Family

I have always spoken highly of the whole Schmitt family, and have related my fond memories of their kindness and generosity to me. When I was a very little boy, Grandma Schmitt always made me my own special birthday cake, just the right size for my age.

Each summer, from the time I was about ten years old through my junior year in high school, I would spend at least one week with my spinster Aunt Viola and bachelor Uncle Harold at the old Schmitt homestead on Fernwood Avenue in Rochester.

Aunt Viola was the oldest child, about age sixty in 1948. She was about five feet tall and very stout, as kind and generous as she was big. She had a jolly, warm disposition and demonstrated an incredible amount of loving patience with the neighbor children while they picked out their penny candy from the many choices in the long candy case in her store.

Aunt Viola ran the neighborhood grocery store, which hadn't changed a light bulb since her father, George, died in ·1925, in the old block within the Schmitt homestead. On the first floor were two stores and an office located off a long hallway that ran from the grocery store to the back of the block. The kitchen also opened off of this hallway. A spacious kitchen with a fifteen-foot ceiling, it featured a huge table for fourteen with chairs as well as a large bench that sat right in front of the hot water radiator.

Above the hot water radiator hung a large picture of the crucifixion of Jesus Christ, something I eventually inherited along with a large picture of the Blessed Mother holding Jesus, which hung in the Schmitt sitting room. An enormous floor-to-ceiling kitchen cabinet held china and pots and pans, and provided food storage. The upper part of the cabinet had glass doors, displaying seven shelves for the china and glassware.

An oversized oval mirror, perhaps eight feet by four feet, hung over the sink. The mirror had been hung at an angle so someone could wash dishes and carry on a face-to-face conversation with the person sitting behind them at the kitchen table. Off the kitchen was a large sitting room located at the rear of the other store. The other store was empty and used for storage.

The stairway going up to the second floor was enormous, about twenty-five steps, five feet wide, with a massive banister. As you ascended the stairs, each step had its own distinct creak that would make you think of a haunted house. Upstairs were ten bedrooms, a large formal dining room, a parlor, a sitting room, an office, a bathroom, and a large reception area at the head of the stairs.

When Grandma Schmitt died in 1947, she was laid out upstairs in the parlor. There were so many beautiful floral pieces that day that they were stacked to the ceiling.

Cousin Rudy Zink recalls that, at that time, he had recently married into Myra Wahl's family. Myra was a grandniece of Grandma Schmitt, and Rudy was asked to be a pallbearer. Not only was Cousin Rudy new to the family, but also it was his first experience as a pallbearer. He said carrying that heavy coffin down that long, steep flight of stairs with the twist at the bottom was an unforgettable experience. Grandma's niece, Marion Aman, remembers the men taking the casket down the steep stairway. Grandma Schmitt was so small, probably seventy-five to eighty pounds at the most, that Marion was sure she must have slid down to the bottom of the coffin.

The funeral procession was huge; it seemed that half the city of Rochester was there to say goodbye to a wonderful, kind, and generous lady.

....

At least once during my summer visits, Aunt Viola and I walked the mile to St. Francis Xavier Church on Bay Street to participate in the "Rosary for Peace," a prayer service for the fall of communism and the conversion of sinners, broadcast live on the radio each night at seven o'clock. She continued to run the now meager and run-down Schmitt grocery store until shortly before her death in 1963.

Uncle Harold was three years younger than Aunt Viola. A very kind, gentle, soft-spoken man, he was about five feet four inches tall, bald and heavy set; he loved to eat.

At that time he worked as a janitor in an apartment building. He would dress in a suit, white shirt, and tie every day, take the bus to work, then change into work clothes. He repeated the process at the end of the day, changing back into his suit before going to dinner in a restaurant downtown. After he ate, he stopped at the YMCA, showered, then went to a movie every night. Then he stopped for a couple of ales at one of Bobby Clifford's restaurants before taking the ten o'clock bus home.

Uncle Harold appeared to be a seasoned traveler; he knew about all the far-flung places in the world and talked at length about all the famous people, the cities, rivers, churches, museums and tourist attractions and the foods in so many countries around the world.

"Uncle Harold, when did you visit all these places?" I asked one day. "It sounds wonderful... Was it when you were in the Army in WWI?"

He replied, "Oh no, George, I never left the USA during the War."

I asked, "Was it right after the War, Uncle Harold?"

"No, George," he told me, "over the years I learned about all these places in many books like the *National Geographic* and you can learn about them too, and maybe someday you will be able to visit them in person if you study hard in school."

Another time I asked him, "Uncle Harold, why didn't you ever marry?"

"Well, George, I never wanted to see a woman work as hard as my mother worked all of her life, and then again, I don't remember any girl asking me to marry her." Then he laughed.

At least once during my visit, he would generally take me on the city bus to dinner on Saturday night, usually to Bobby Clifford's restaurant, and to a movie in downtown Rochester.

My Uncle Tony Schmitt, a bachelor, was fifty-five years old at the time my summer visits began. About six feet tall, medium build and bald, he had a big smile and a hearty hello. He lived above Schmitt's horseradish processing and bottling shop. I don't remember Uncle Tony ever having a regular job, just sort of working here and there; he was a free-spirited individual living day to day, seemingly with not a care in the world.

The shop was located in front of the barn that formerly housed the horse-drawn delivery wagons on the Schmitt homestead, where Uncle Tony sometimes made horseradish, bottled it under the family label, "Green Label Horseradish," and sold it to hotels in the Rochester area as the Schmitt family had done for many years.

Uncle Tony was a lot of fun to be with; he was a kid at heart. He often took me in his black 1934 Packard convertible roadster with a rumble seat to Sea Breeze, an amusement park, where we rode all the rides together. Once we went on a big ferryboat from Buffalo across Lake Erie to Crystal Beach, an amusement park in Canada, and we rode all the rides together.

Another time he took me to see the Canadian Expo in Toronto for a whole week. There were four huge Ferris wheels in a row. What a ball we had going through all the exhibits! Ma would never have let me go if she knew we slept in the car.

Uncle Tony would come to Mumford several times during the year and take us kids and the neighborhood children to a dairy in Limerock for ice cream. It was the best ice cream in the world, and they had a zillion flavors and waffle cones. Sometimes, on the way back home we would· stop at Butter Milk Falls and climb down the very steep hill to the bottom of the waterfalls.

Uncle Leo, who was forty-six, and Uncle Neal, age fifty-eight, lived next door to each other with their wives and families on Portage Street, one street away from the Schmitt homestead. They were both short men, slightly built and bald. They were very kind and always had time for me. Both were carpenters and they each built their own homes; together they took care of all the maintenance on the Schmitt homestead.

Sometimes Uncle Neal would take me in his Model A Ford open-air truck to the Rochester Public Market on Saturday mornings to sell flowers, giving me a chance to earn some spending money. At noon, the Public Market closed and we returned to Uncle Neal's home where we shared a meal with Aunt Eleanor and their small children, Neal and Ann.

I remember Uncle Leo taking my cousin, Bobby DuBois, and me fishing in his boat at nearby Irondequoit Bay and swimming at his cottage on the shore of Lake Ontario. After swimming, Uncle Leo treated us at Don and Bob's open-air stand to hot dogs, sodas and custard ice cream. What fun we had!

Uncle George, three years younger than Uncle Leo, was also short, about five feet two inches, of slight build and bald. He too spoke softly and was a very kind man. He and his wife, Lena, and three daughters, Theresa, Sophia, and Caroline, lived about a mile away from the Schmitt homestead on Clifford Avenue.

He sometimes took me with him to his part-time flower farm where he grew a hundred thousand gladiolas; he gave me an opportunity to work at weeding to earn some spending money. On the way home, Uncle George would always stop at his favorite watering hole and restaurant on Goodman Street and buy me a hamburger and soda.

Aunt Caroline DuBois, the youngest of the Schmitt daughters, and my godmother, was about forty-seven when I began my summer visits to the Schmitts. She would come a long way across town by bus just to visit with me. Petite, with blond hair and blue eyes, she was one of my favorites, very kind and generous to me, a very loving aunt who always made a big fuss each time we visited and especially so for all the holidays. On my eighteenth birthday, when I was living at the YMCA, she sent me a telegram to wish me a happy birthday; back then telegrams were still delivered by young men on bicycles.

············

I will never forget how the Schmitt family always had time for me, were happy to see me, and always made me feel welcome and special. However, I never experienced any such joy with the Zeller side of the family. My memories of my Zeller grandparents were people who were not friendly, just drab.

In 1948, Grandpa Walter Stanley Zeller was sixty-nine years old; he was about five feet two inches tall, with a stocky build, on the heavy side. He was bald except for a rim of gray hair, and wore rimmed bifocal glasses. He no longer worked at the shoe factory and was now working as a janitor in a nearby church. By nature he was a silent man and didn't smile often. He seemed preoccupied, deep in thought, and I was of little interest to him; he rarely spoke to me.

Grandma Florence Zeller had gray hair and brown eyes; she was of medium build and just two inches shorter than her husband. She too wore bifocal glasses with silver rims. She seldom smiled and scowled often; she seemed always to be in a grouchy mood and was negative about everything. Her squeaky voice was noticeable and it amplified when she complained about some member of the family—and there was always someone on her list.

I don't remember them displaying any affection or joy of any kind... no hugs, and rarely was I even called by name. I don't recall ever receiving a birthday card or a Christmas present. I really don't remember ever being pleasantly acknowledged that I was even alive by my Zeller grandparents.

Grandma and Grandpa Zeller, 1954.

When my parents would visit, I sat in a chair by myself and patiently waited in my quiet world for the grown-up conversation to be completed so we could go home. There was never an offer of a cookie, crackers, or a glass of milk or a piece of candy. But worst of all, I experienced the feeling of not being welcome in their home.

I longed to feel welcome, longed for their warmth, friendship and happiness, all of which were absent, yet were so abundant and so freely given on the Schmitt side of the family. I felt my Zeller grandparents practiced to the fullest the belief: kids should be seen and not heard. I dreaded each visit.

For as long as I can remember while growing up, there always seemed to be tension in the air among the Zellers. This eerie low-key uncomfortable feeling had a lasting and profound effect on me. It would be more than fifty years later, while involved in genealogy research with my eighty-two-year-old widowed Aunt Laura Zeller Chase, that I would accidentally learn the most likely cause of their sour and drab disposition—and a whole lot more, unraveling a mystery in my life.

CHAPTER VI

Growing Up Early

The final blow to Pa's hope of being a gentleman farmer came with his realization in 1949 that his eleven-year-old son (myself) had developed a serious asthmatic condition and could not work in the dust on the farm. My older brother had graduated from high school in 1948 and moved on to Rochester. Without the free labor of the next drudge, me, there was no way Pa could pursue his dream.

I often thought, as I grew considerably taller than Walter, that Pa's frustrations must have grown right along with me. At that time Pa was still trying to operate the farm with a team of work horses and the equipment from the turn of the century. Subsequently, in about 1950, Pa finally accepted the crowning blow and sold the horses and livestock, and stored all the horse-drawn farm equipment in the barn.

....

I recall vividly that during the wee hours of the morning whenever I had a very bad asthma attack and was gasping for air that my mother sat up with me. She would rub my back upward in a circular motion by the hour as I sat in a kitchen chair with my head resting on pillows on the kitchen table.

Over and over Ma would say, "You're okay, George... you will be fine, just relax." As she rubbed my back, her hands had such a calming and soothing effect that often I was able to fall asleep and get some much needed rest. I remember, when these attacks went on for several days, many times waking up with my mother sitting next to me asleep with her head resting on the kitchen table.

I was very much aware during these asthma attacks that my father seemed to avoid me. He never came into my room; he never asked me how I was doing. Pa never once tried to console me. I thought that my father didn't like me, as it seemed entirely my fault that Pa was not able to continue to operate the farm, and these feelings gnawed at me and troubled me for many years.

. . . .

In the late fall and winter, from the time I was eleven until I was fifteen, Pa and I cut down the long row of old apple trees and sawed up the trees for firewood. The apple trees, located just beyond the double set of elevated railroad tracks about a quarter a mile away from the barns, were no longer producing quality apples; their fruit now tasted woody.

During these years, on Saturday and Sunday afternoons, we would cut up the trees with a two-man saw. Pa taught me how to use a bucksaw on the smaller limbs and how to split the logs using a wedge or two and the sledgehammer. We also cut down the apple tree by the barn on Armstrong Road, the big elm tree, and many other trees that needed thinning in the hedgerows on the farm. The elm trees were the hardest to saw; they were like ironwood. I quickly learned that the logs split much more easily when they were frozen.

It was my job to haul the firewood home and stack it in the wood shed after school during the week. Before the snow fell I used a wheelbarrow and, when the snow was a couple of inches deep, a toboggan to transport the firewood home. I generally made two trips each night after school. Often I would recruit the help of my friends, and they would bring their toboggans or carts so that in one trip we could bring back several loads of firewood and my work would be done early, so everyone could play basketball in the barn.

As the house was heated with wood, I quickly learned the importance of keeping the cellar well supplied with dry, seasoned firewood. Since Pa worked nights, it was my job to bank the furnace with firewood each evening before going to bed so the fire didn't go out before morning.

Mary Ann and George, 1952

CHAPTER VII

Adolescence and Adversity

When I was fourteen years old, in my sophomore year of high school, Ma was often depressed and would have migraine headaches for days on end. She would often lie down in the afternoon or after supper and place a damp cold washcloth on her forehead. Many days she had very little to say and she cried a lot.

I had no idea what was going on. I just thought she was having problems dealing with Pa's harshness, just like I was. In later years, I realized that Ma then was fifty-one years old and probably had been going through the change of life for some time.

....

In the early spring of 1953, I told Pa, "I need a new pair of shoes—see, my socks are showing through the sides of my shoes." I tried repeatedly to get him to listen.

Each time, Pa replied, "Yeah, yeah, that's the way it is. Money doesn't grow on trees."

Then one evening, I overheard Ma and Pa talking and learned that he had not given Ma the weekly house money from his paycheck. I got into a horrendous argument with Pa, and Ma cried, "Pa, George, stop, stop!"

I surprised Pa with my quickness and strength and physically put him on the floor. Ma was crying and begged for me to stop. I took his wallet out of his pants pocket, took the money out of his wallet, and gave it to Ma. There was considerably more money in the wallet than the house money.

I had Pa's arm bent behind his back and my knee in his back. Before I let him up, I made him promise he would buy me a pair of shoes. I didn't hit him with my fist or hurt him in any way except for his pride.

After I let Pa up, he ran to a neighbor, the McKeons' house, and telephoned the sheriff's office. He didn't come back into the house until the sheriff arrived. Pa was telling the sheriff his side of the story, as Ma cried and corrected Pa's story.

"Pa, tell the truth," she said.

In the end, in front of the sheriff, Pa agreed to buy me a new pair of shoes, and I agreed that I would never get physical with him again. Pa gave me money to buy the cheapest pair of shoes that Thom McCann Shoe Store sold, as advertised in the newspaper. After that the tension between us continued to fester, and there was no let up in sight.

1951 - George, 13, Mary Ann, 16, Otillia (Ma), 49, and Walter Zeller, 21 years old, a corporal in the USMC

....

For some time now I had felt something wasn't right with my mother. She was often sad and cried a lot.

I knew she was worried sick about Walter, since he joined the Marine Corps in the summer of 1950 shortly after the outbreak of the Korean War. He had been stationed in

Hawaii for some time now and we knew that most likely he would be shipped out to the front lines in Korea.

I heard Ma say, "Pa, sit down and write your son Walter a letter. You haven't sent him one letter since he went in the service; God forbid you may never see him again."

Pa replied, "You write the letters; I don't have the time."

"I don't know why you act like that," said Ma. "Walter is your son and he is a long way from home—what is the matter with you?"

Pa didn't answer her, and he never did write a letter to Walter during the four years he was in the service.

I remember talking with my brother later on about his basic training in the USMC. "Walter, I heard it is very tough in basic training and they have forced marches through the swamps," I said. "And in the newspaper it said a couple of the guys hung themselves with their belts in the latrine... Is it true?"

He replied, "Yes, it's true; it is very tough physically and mentally in basic training. They treat you like you're a dog, like you're nothing—just like Pa does."

"Were you afraid when they hollered at you to do something?"

"No, I just thought of Pa when he hollered at me. Heck, Pa was tougher than any drill sergeant I had. That's all I had to do when the going got real tough, just think of Pa and whatever I was doing was a piece of cake," said Walter, with a grim expression on his face.

"It got to be a game with me, George, but it got me through some real tough stuff."

He went on, "Don't ever forget it—whenever you think that whatever you are doing is real tough, just think of Pa, and you will laugh it off and you will be okay. There is nothing wrong with being afraid, but just keep your head about you and keep moving along and it will pass. Do you understand, George?"

"Yes, I think so; I will remember what you said."

....

Aunt Caroline DuBois, Ma's youngest sister, and her husband, Bill, were favorites of mine, and for years I had great times with my cousins Bobby and Jimmy DuBois. Our families would get together at each other's homes with some regularity. Generally, these family affairs were in the afternoons and ran into the evenings, with fun and plenty of food and sodas. The aunts and uncles would play cards, usually Pinochle, and the children played games and sports as weather permitted.

When Bobby turned fourteen, we sometimes went to the bowling alley on Dewey Avenue in Rochester. We were in the same grade in school, but I was about eleven months younger than Bobby. Jimmy, who was several years older than Bobby, often went off to do things with his older friends. Bobby and I always had great times together, laughing and teasing each other, and looked forward to these family get-togethers.

However, in 1953, for reasons unknown to me, quite suddenly Uncle Bill and Aunt Caroline separated. The happy family times that Bobby and I had grown accustomed to were gone and were replaced with sadness, stress, and uncertainty. In 1954, Bobby and I were in our junior year in high school; he attended John Marshall High School in Rochester.

I recall conversations with Bobby, who confided in me about the dire financial condition his family was in. He worked most evenings after school and weekends setting pins at a bowling alley to help his mother with the family expenses. He was sad and tried to put up a good front, but it showed through that it was affecting him.

One day at school after lunch, in February 1954, Bobby went to gym class. The class was learning to wrestle and the boys were paired off. During Bobby's wrestling match, he choked on his lunch, and collapsed. Everyone kept saying, "Get up, Bobby, stop fooling around—you're not hurt. Quit faking, and get up."

He never regained consciousness, and died on the mat in the gym, much to the shock and horror of his classmates and teacher. This was a tragedy for the family and friends, and a terrible loss for me. Again I was called upon to be a pallbearer for a cousin and a very close friend. It had been only seven years since my cousin Jimmy McCombs had been killed while riding his bicycle home from school.

....

After the labor strike at Ebsary Gypsum mine, Pa got a job at Lapp Insulator Company in LeRoy about seven miles away, and later he worked at the JELL-O Company, also in LeRoy. Pa had generally worked the "B" shift, three-thirty p.m. to midnight, or "C" shift, eleven-thirty p.m. to eight a.m.

In the summer of 1954, just before the beginning of my senior year in high school, Pa went to work at Gerber Baby Food in Rochester, working days. He was home by four o'clock in the afternoon, and my life turned really bad. My father controlled everything; he eliminated all of my freedoms and set rigid rules and some ridiculous chores. He kept enlarging the yard; it was well over an acre for me to cut each week as it was, and now Pa increased it a little bit more each week.

I had to be in bed, lights out by ten on school nights because Pa went to bed at ten during the week. I had to be home by ten-thirty on Friday nights after the games, which were barely over by ten-fifteen; I was always late, and the next day I always caught a raft from Pa.

He controlled the TV; we watched only the programs that he wanted to see and then he would turn the TV off. He was on my case from the time I got home from school until bedtime.

One day after school when his bullying had been especially bad, I said, "Pa, I think you are totally unreasonable. You're nasty with your restrictions and demands, and there is no reason for you to be acting like this towards me."

Pa yelled, "Boy, don't you ever speak to me again in that tone of voice! I am your father and this is my house; I make the rules, and if you don't abide by my rules, I will call the sheriff, boy. They have a place for kids like you who don't want to obey, called INDUSTRY!"

I knew where Industry was and I did not want to be sent there; it was a detention home for delinquents. I also remembered what the sheriff said when I got into it with Pa over a pair of shoes.

Ma tried to intervene, saying, "Don't be so strict; George isn't doing anything wrong."

"Stay out of it," Pa replied. "I'm going to teach him a lesson. He is going to obey me, and do what I tell him to do, period."

Ma looked at me and rolled her eyes. "George, he is your father; you better do what he says or there's going to be trouble."

Then Pa would stare at me and not say a word. He loved to give me the silent treatment; sometimes this would go on for several weeks. I remembered what my brother said to me about the drill sergeant in basic training in the Marines—"He will treat you like a dog, but he's not as tough as Pa"—and I sometimes would laugh to myself; but deep inside I wondered why Pa did these things to me.

I was not afraid of him and he knew that. I think that really bugged my father, knowing he could not rattle my cage, but I always remembered the sheriff's words. I also remembered what Ma said, "George, be sure you remember the Fourth Commandment, 'Honor both your mother and your father!'"

My senior year, 1954-1955, was a living hell. I vividly remember how Pa could become cantankerous without any cause. When my friends and I wanted to play basketball in the barn, he regularly refused to back his car out of the barn or to allow us to push the car out. Arbitrarily, he acted this way about many things and embarrassed me over and over again while my friends were present.

My close friend, Charley Daniels, whose father had been killed in WWII and who was usually quite reserved for his age, expressed himself after one of these encounters: "Your mom is so terrific, but your father is miserable and obnoxious. He is so unreasonable; he doesn't make any sense."

●●●●●●●●●●●●

My father, Walter Cecil Zeller, at age about 49
April 1903—February 1985

In my senior year I practiced and tried out for the high school varsity basketball team over about a two-week period, and it had been indicated that I would make the team. I was so happy and excited and could not wait to tell Ma and Pa that it looked like I was going to make the team.

Pa announced, "George, you can practice, but you are not allowed to play basketball in any school games."

That finished basketball, but I have to admit that I wasn't very good at the sport; most likely I would have just sat on the bench at the games. I sure did miss being a part of the team, though, as Caledonia-Mumford Central School was the county basketball champ in 1954-1955 and advanced to the regional semi-finals. Sadly, I was not part of the team and its triumph.

Tennis was different: just show up and you were on the team. Why Pa let me play tennis, I don't know. I played and lettered in my junior and senior years. Pa would laugh and say, "George, that is a sissy sport. Why would you want to play a sissy sport?

"Pa, it's not as easy as you think, you should try it." But Pa only laughed.

In my senior year I remember coming home with great excitement after I had won each of my first three matches, but I received no comment from Pa. However, after I lost the next three matches, Pa commented each time, "You're not as good as you thought you were," and after the third loss he said, "Well, that's three losses in a row; I think that makes you even." I never again told Pa the results of the tennis matches, and finished the season seven wins and three losses.

My school marks were terrible; barely sliding through each year had become a way of life. To keep the peace at home, I changed the marks on the report card. After Pa or Ma signed the first ten-week report card, I told the school I had lost the report card while bringing it back to school. I lied, of course. The report card was on the top shelf in my locker at school. Then, when the next report card came out and each time thereafter, I signed it and returned it the next day.

In the meantime, I filled in the report card that I kept in my locker with average marks that suggested I had studied and took it home for my parents to sign. Pa thought surely he had straightened me out in school. If I had only understood how I was hurting myself, I might have adjusted my attitude.

CHAPTER VIII

Life Would Never Be the Same

In the late spring of 1955, my world collapsed. I was walking home from school, and as usual smoking a cigarette. As I came over the brink of the hill at the beginning of Armstrong Road, I could see the flashing red lights of several emergency vehicles in the neighborhood of our house; perhaps twelve hundred feet away.

I began to jog, and as I got closer I could see that the emergency vehicles were parked right in front of our home; and then the white ambulance was leaving with its red light flashing and siren blaring. The lights on the fire department and sheriff's vehicles were also flashing.

Racing into our yard, I thought, "Oh my God, what's wrong... what's wrong... what has happened?" As I approached my father I hollered, "Pa, what is it... what happened?"

"Ma tried to commit suicide by taking an overdose of sleeping pills and she is being taken in the ambulance to Strong Memorial Hospital in Rochester," he said.

At first, I could not believe it—not Ma—she wouldn't do this, not Ma. The sheriff stayed a few more minutes writing his report and then left about the same time as the volunteers in the fire department.

Ma stayed in the hospital for a couple of weeks in what was called the mental ward at that time, and then was sent home. A few weeks passed and things appeared perhaps a little quieter than normal, but not alarming.

Then early one dreary, rainy Saturday morning, when Pa awoke, he could not find Ma in the house or in the barn. He woke me up about five a.m. and said, "Ma's missing; she's not in the house. I'm going to go look for her in the cedar woods." The cedar woods were across the railroad tracks and over the hill near the far end of the forty-eight-acre farm.

I jumped out of bed, hurriedly put on my clothes and shoes, and dashed out the door. First I looked upstairs in the chicken coop, then throughout the barn, in the silo, milk house, woodshed, and smoke house.

It was drizzling now, and the fog was thick as I looked down the hill towards the creek. I decided to look there as Ma was very fond of the creek and she liked to sit on a log under a large tree with a white trunk. She enjoyed watching the fast current of the trout stream as it flowed swiftly into the deep swimming hole that we enjoyed for so many years. The water seemed to slow as it gently moved through the old swimming hole because the creek was a bit wider and deeper at that spot; then the water quickly picked up speed as the creek became shallow and shortly would reach a large bend before there was another sharp turn in the creek.

I ran down Livermore's hill and across Baker's cow pasture toward the creek. The closer I got to the creek the denser the fog became and it was now as thick as soup. I found the bend in the creek and walked along its bank towards the swimming hole. In a little while, I found Ma in the water in Oatka Creek, by the old swimming hole. She was trying to commit suicide by drowning.

When I finally got her out of the creek, I looked into her glassy eyes and asked, "Ma, why are you doing this?"

She replied, "I don't know why, George. I don't know why."

I put my arms around my mother, and we both cried and then walked home together in the drizzling rain, hand in hand, through the wet, cold, tall grass, both crying all the way home.

About seven a.m. Pa came home from the far end of our farm. He was soaking wet, and called Doctor Hare at his home. Doctor Hare came to our house and examined Ma. He told us there was nothing physically wrong with her and, unfortunately, there was nothing he could do for her, as he was not trained in psychiatry.

Doctor Hare thought she should be taken back to Strong Memorial Hospital and offered to take us in his car, as he was on his way to the hospital to make his rounds of his patients there; Pa accepted. I was bitterly angry with Doctor Hare. The doctor was my friend, but he couldn't help Ma. He could always fix anything before this.

After Doctor Hare had admitted Ma to the hospital, Pa and I walked from Strong Memorial Hospital to Grandpa Zeller's house on Brooks Avenue. It must have been two or three miles, and Pa cried most of the way. This was the first time I had ever seen my father hurt inside; he was so gentle and spoke very softly as he sobbed. When we reached Grandpa's home, Pa's brother Kenny gave us a ride in his car back to Mumford.

Shortly thereafter, Ma was moved to the New York State Mental Hospital on South Avenue in Rochester.

Visiting hours were only on Wednesday and Sunday from two-thirty to four p.m. The hospital grounds included many old, large two-story red brick buildings with large porches that could accommodate perhaps forty people, with rocking chairs as well as straight chairs. The porches were screened and barred like a jail, for security.

In order to visit Ma, it was necessary to sign in. Then a matron would unlock and relock the first of a series of three large heavy security doors. After we passed through the first security door, we entered a corridor about thirty feet long with no windows and very high ceilings, perhaps fifteen feet high, and were taken to the second security door. The matron unlocked this door and we entered a hallway where two doctors' offices were on one side. Each office was stark white with no pictures or diplomas on the walls; there was just a small desk and one or two chairs. After passing these offices, the matron unlocked the third large door that led into a fairly large ward.

The ward's main sitting room was sparsely furnished, the furniture limited primarily to rocking chairs and wicker chairs. It would accommodate approximately fifty women. The sleeping area was in a barracks-style room off the sitting room. The women ranged in age from approximately forty to about sixty-five years of age. There were hundreds of women in the hospital.

The visits with Ma would range from five to thirty minutes, but generally about fifteen minutes was long enough for Ma, and quite often she was apprehensive or had very little awareness that I was there; she seemed so far away. On many occasions my visit was very short. I felt terrible for her, but nothing I could say to her would make her smile.

It was near the end of my senior year in high school, in early June. I was sixteen years old and devastated about Ma and angry toward Pa. I was completely lost, embarrassed and alone, with no one to talk to. I felt ashamed for something I had nothing to do with, and I did not understand. I was confused, to say the least, with all of this bottled up inside me.

No one outside of the immediate family had any idea what was going on with my mother. I was made to feel that this was a disgrace in our family, and not a word should ever be spoken of Ma's condition outside of our home—it's not an illness, it's a disgrace and it brings shame to our family.

•••••••••••

My English teacher, Russell Reed, was about forty years old, a tall, frail man with a thin face and dark brown straight hair with no wave or style to it. He loved Shakespeare and poetry and often read to the class from "Romeo and Juliet." Generally I couldn't figure out what he was talking about. His lanky frame reminded our class of Ichabod Crane, who met the headless horseman in the "Legend of Sleepy Hollow" by Washington Irving. Often one of the classmates would pull his shirt up over his head and try to imitate the dangling arms of the headless horseman.

Mr. Reed dressed smartly but differently from the other male teachers; he seemed to be in his own private world—a teacher you might think of as teaching in an Ivy League boarding school. He dressed in either a green or black double-breasted tweed suit with a white shirt, a vest and a brightly colored silk argyle tie. Sometimes he wore a gray tweed sport coat and a vest, but always wore a brightly colored tie; a pocket watch with a gold chain was attached to his vest. As neatly as he dressed, it was odd that his shoes were rarely shined.

A kind, gentle man who loved to teach, Mr. Reed had reached out several times trying to help me as the school year was ending, but watched me reject and ignore all his efforts. He repeatedly tried so hard to be a real friend to me; but I was blind to the realization of what was actually happening. My mind was closed to the reality of this moment and I just didn't care about school.

I was deeply troubled, all bottled up inside and consumed with my anguish, unable to set my home life aside for the moment; yet never would I say a word of it to anyone, and no one knew what had happened. Mr. Reed went one step further, and secured approval for me to take the New York State Regents Exam for English, which I had no right to take.

He said, "George, if you can just get a grade of sixty-five on this test you can graduate with your class." Instead of trying hard to pass the exam, I walked out of the final test with no attempt to answer the last two ten-point essay questions. Mr. Reed did what he needed to do; he failed me, with a score of sixty-one. I was so immature!

Ma was now in the New York State Hospital. I no longer feared my father; I knew he was my father, but I also recognized that he was just a man. I arose each morning at four-thirty a.m. to get Pa's breakfast, and make his lunch before he left for work at five-thirty. I took over most of Ma's chores of the household and did the washing of the clothes on the back porch using the old wringer washing machine and hung the clothes on the line by the wood shed, did the ironing and the house work, made supper and did the dishes, using all of the knowledge of taking care of a home that Ma had taught me when I was twelve years old, when I thought I would never turn thirteen. I went to summer school at Monroe High School in Rochester to study English.

My mode of transportation was hitchhiking and this is how I met Mr. Beech, the father of Phemie Beech, a high school classmate and friend of mine. He picked me up on his way to work as I walked towards the main road, Route 383, near the twin bridges over Oatka Creek. Mr. Beech, a kind man about sixty years old, recognized my situation and generously gave me a free ride each day to the corner of Main and Alexander streets about five blocks from the high school. He even picked me up at my home each morning. Pa gave me enough spending money to take the bus from Main Street to Genesee Valley Park where I could hitchhike a ride the twenty-five miles home.

While attending summer school, Pa asked me to visit Grandpa Zeller in Genesee Hospital on Alexander Street. So I stopped after class on my walk to catch the bus. He was recovering from a heart attack that he had suffered perhaps a week before. It was a hot day in August and Grandpa Zeller, now seventy-five, was lying in bed, in a large ward without the benefit of air conditioning, with perhaps ten other sick men.

I was surprised how friendly he was. He smiled and seemed genuinely happy to see me, and was interested in talking with me; we talked for about twenty minutes. I thought that was nice, but so strange as we had never talked before. He died about two days later, on August 11, 1955.

During this six-week period of summer school, Pa acted very different than ever before. He was withdrawn, spoke softly with a gentle voice, didn't give me orders or holler at me, and he even asked me several times, "George, do you need any money for bus fare or spending money?"

Often I said, "No, Pa, I have enough for now." If I needed additional money, I asked Pa for it, and he gave it to me with no hassle at all. I was relieved and thought this pleasantness was really nice, but wondered inside, pondered and thought, when would the father that I knew resurface and come suddenly back into my life.

In summer school, the class was given the assignment to read a book, *Fortitude*, by Hugh Walpole. It was about courage, and it helped me greatly through a very difficult time in my life. I no longer can recall the name of the teacher, who came from John Marshall High School in Rochester, the school where my cousin Bobby had died in a wrestling accident.

The teacher was excellent; he was kind and patient but demanded effort. This teacher never made me feel dumb or ignorant or that I was a screw-up or a failure. We were just there to learn, and each day was a fresh, new day. I passed English with an above-ninety mark and received my diploma by mid-August.

CHAPTER IX
Leaving Home

I had just turned seventeen in July 1955, had grown up a little bit, and had changed my attitude a great deal. Ma had recently been released from the New York State Hospital and returned home.

Now I was on my way; with my high school diploma in hand I was ready for the world of employment! At the New York State Employment Office I was interviewed and then during the next week I was sent out several times to different companies for a job, but was unsuccessful.

Eventually they sent me to Dun & Bradstreet on the fourteenth floor in the Temple Building in downtown Rochester to be interviewed. I got the job as a Multilith operator for D&B and would be taught how to print their commercial credit reports. Boy, was I excited—I couldn't wait to get home to tell my parents. I took the city bus out to Route 383, stuck out my thumb and got lucky; I caught a ride all the way to Mumford and just a short walk home.

I remember how happy, proud, and excited I was as I ran into the house hollering; "Ma, Pa, guess what, guess what? I got a job, a fulltime job at Dun & Bradstreet, starting at $125 per month; and I start tomorrow!"

Pa rose from his chair, turned slowly towards me, set his feet, crossed his arms and glared at me as only he could, then replied in a loud snarling voice, "YOU WON'T LAST TWO WEEKS!"

He surprised me, but it only lasted a moment, and I replied, "Oh yes, I will, Pa; I'll show you; I know how to work hard—remember, Pa, you taught me!"

My father, the old cantankerous Pa, was back, the one I knew so well; he had returned with a vengeance. Never again, during the balance of his life, would I experience the gentleness within him that I had enjoyed so much during the six weeks of summer school.

A few moments later, once again the lion roared, "Now that you will be working, room and board is $15 per week, and that is every week."

"Okay, Pa," I said.

Once again, I arranged for a ride, this time to go to work, with Mr. Beech, who had given me a free ride to summer school. I paid him $5 a week. He picked me up at six-forty a.m. at the house. In the afternoon, after work, I took the city bus out to meet him on Plymouth Avenue for the ride home. We got home about six-thirty each evening. My weekly room and board was $15, and I only grossed $29 per week, but was paid twice monthly. After paying for my ride to work, lunches and coffee breaks, there was little money left to buy anything else.

I soon realized there was nothing to do in Mumford on weekends, and I was bored—and broke all of the time. My relationship with Pa was unbearable. He continued to be critical of everything I said or did; he acted as though he couldn't wait for me to get fired.

Keeping my father's negative comments and attitude in mind toward my future success, I worked at D&B each day with a zest, determination, and commitment to succeed beyond anything that I had known before. I was confident that the work ethic that my father had instilled in me, with the emphasis on attention to detail, would see me through.

Ma's health was about the same; she was very quiet and withdrawn most of the time. It was sad to see her that way.

....

About two months later I decided to move out. My sister, Mary Ann, was married by now, and my brother-in-law, Frank Kosakowski, drove out to Mumford and helped me move my clothes out of the house to a room at the YMCA on Gibbs Street in Rochester. I paid $7 a week for a room on the seventh floor, small, but perfect, by my standards.

It was pleasant at the Y. There was a coffee shop and cafeteria, a barbershop, pool tables, TV area, gym, basketball court, handball courts, track, weight room, and a swimming pool. It was just a five-minute walk to my job at Dun & Bradstreet. Nearby there were department stores to browse in, several movie theaters, a library, St. Joseph's Catholic Church, and free recitals by the students at the Eastman School of Music available almost every evening in Kilbourne Hall, all within easy walking distance.

I ate supper most evenings right after work at the White Swan Restaurant on Main Street. Each night the menu featured a One-Dollar Special that included soup, salad, entree, bread and butter, dessert and a beverage. The owner must have taken a liking to me, because he always gave me large portions and I always ate it all. My favorite special on the menu was the hamburger steak smothered with onions, with mashed potatoes and gravy.

I was in heaven, free of the tension and daily criticism from my father. I was accepted and happy at work, and pleased with my new life and myself. However, a short time later, particularly in the evenings, I realized I was very lonely. Since money was always short for entertainment, I found myself at evening church services at St. Joseph's Catholic Church three and four nights a week. I was comfortable in church, very much at home and at peace, and my loneliness seemed to disappear.

Now, money management was a lesson that I had not learned yet; a lesson that I was about to learn. A few weeks after moving into the Y, I had met some new people, went to dinner and a movie, both on Saturday and Sunday nights, splurged for the first time on my own, and had a really great weekend, a lot of fun and laughs. On Monday morning, I woke up, got ready as usual for work, and then transferred my loose change, keys, and wallet to my work pants. In doing so I realized I had a total of $3.50 left to my name, and payday was not until Friday at noon. How was I going to eat for four and a half days?

By Wednesday night I was almost broke and hungry; I remember sitting in a tall chair by the pool tables that were adjacent to the coffee shop in the YMCA. The smell of the hamburgers and fried onions cooking on the grill was enough to make me drool. I awoke Thursday morning starved, with just twenty-five cents left to my name, but it was enough for a cup of coffee and two glazed donuts.

At work I tentatively approached Harriett Long, a friend I had made at work. Harriett was the mother hen of the office, a well-to-do, kind-hearted lady who watched over the flock; a spinster, about fifty years old, she had worked at D&B for twenty-five years. I asked Harriett if I could please borrow $2 until tomorrow, payday.

Without hesitation, she handed me a $5 bill, and said, "Take this, George."

"Thank you, thank you, Harriett!"

On Friday at noon, I cashed my check and paid Harriett back the $5 and thanked her again from the bottom of my heart. That scene would be repeated time and time again with loans gradually increasing to $20.

Then one Friday before a holiday weekend with payday the following Tuesday, Harriett came over to me and asked, "Are you okay for this long weekend or can I help you?"

"Thank you, Harriett, I think I am going to be okay." I only had $6 left, but I had finally realized that I was always going to be short of funds, if I didn't stop borrowing. I needed to make do, and tough it out with what I had in my pocket. It sure felt great when I got paid on the following Tuesday and didn't have a loan to pay back. Harriett and I were good friends for many years; I will always remember her kindness to me. A hard lesson on money management—I finally learned and never forgot!

During these years, Mary Ann and her husband, Frank, were kind and generous to me, and we spent many evenings and weekends together. I enjoyed them and appreciated their company and hospitality. I always felt that I was welcome in their home and had the pleasure to being part of their family during the early years when three of their children, Frank, Judy, and Steve, were born.

My brother-in-law, Frank, a factory worker, stood almost six feet tall and had a beautiful full head of dark brown hair. He was a handsome man, an excellent dresser, and even dressed up for his job in the factory. Frank had a warm, outgoing personality, and he was a great friend to me when I desperately needed a friend in 1955, 1956 and 1957.

I was grateful to him for helping me get settled at the Y, but that had not set too well with Pa. It certainly didn't score any brownie points for Frank either.

When I was seventeen and living at the Y, I asked Pa to sign his approval, so I could get a driver's learning permit, and Pa roared as he told me, "NO." So I waited eight more months, and on my eighteenth birthday I got my permit; I no longer needed Pa's permission. I never considered asking Pa to help me get a loan when I bought my first car. As a matter of fact, I never asked Pa for anything after that.

....

In the spring of 1956, the farm in Mumford was sold, and Ma and Pa began the process of moving to Rochester. After the furniture was moved out, they were cleaning up the house, and about six o'clock, a neighbor girl, Maureen Livermore, made a terrible discovery. She found that Ma had removed the boards over the old well that were covered with a thin coat of cement, and had leaped into the forty-foot well, the one that received the raw sewage from the toilet.

Maureen alerted Pa and her father, Harold Livermore, who called the sheriff's office and the Mumford Volunteer Fire Department. A volunteer fireman was lowered into the well and got Ma out. The old well had been made to look as though it was still an operating well with the old pump in place. The perimeter around the pump was decorated with the same greenery that had always been there.

Miraculously, Ma was not killed, although she suffered some facial cuts and body bruises. The ambulance took her back to the New York State Hospital, where her condition was reported later that evening as "fair."

As planned, Pa moved in temporarily with my Aunt Viola and Uncle Harold, in the old Schmitt homestead in Rochester. After a while, Ma would sometimes get a weekend pass from the hospital. Pa would pick her up on Friday afternoon and take her back on Sunday. Several months passed before Pa bought a small, two-bedroom house on Hinchey Road in Chili, just outside the Rochester city limits.

．．．．．．．．．．．．

I moved back home in the late fall of 1956 for awhile, in part to try to save some money to buy a car, and also in hopes that my presence would help Ma somewhat. Within a month after moving back home, I found a part-time job at Security Trust Bank filing checks in the evenings and on one or two Saturdays each month.

I was soon sorry I had moved back home. Living at the Y, both my job at D&B and my part-time job were within ten minutes walking time. But it would have been awkward to move back to the Y now, as Ma seemed sometimes to enjoy having me around.

One afternoon in early 1957, Ma was having a good day; she was sharp as a tack and tried to express herself to Pa about how she felt then, and about the desperate needs in her life that were pent up inside of her and bursting to be heard. To my knowledge Ma had never pleaded like this before. I recall hearing the agitation in her voice as she talked with Pa.

"Pa, let's rent a cottage this summer on Lake Conesus for a week and go swimming and enjoy the water; or drive around the wine trails along the back roads and visit some of the vineyards in the Finger Lakes area. Maybe we could take a tour of the wineries in Naples or in Hammondsport, or take a ride up to the Thousand Islands on the St. Lawrence River, or drive to Lake Seneca."

Getting no response, she added, "Pa, all these places are within one hundred and fifty miles of home."

He raised his voice angrily and growled, "I need to paint the trim and the gutters on the house on my vacation this year."

"Pa, do you remember our last vacation together was in 1929? It was our two-night honeymoon—we spent our wedding night at the Hotel Rochester and the second night in Niagara Falls; we had to return your father's car so he could go to work."

He just stared at her, his face hard.

Ma almost screamed in frustration, "My last vacation away from home was in 1948 with the kids, because you wouldn't go with us"

After receiving her inheritance money in 1948 from her mother's estate, that summer Ma had taken Mary Ann and me on our first airplane ride from Rochester to Buffalo. We spent four nights at the Hotel Statler there, and we took the bus from Buffalo to Lackawanna to visit Father Baker's Orphanage, and Our Lady of Victory Basilica and the National Shrine. The following day we visited the Buffalo Zoo, and on the last day we took the steamer, the *Canadiana*, across Lake Erie, to the Crystal Beach Amusement Park in Canada.

My mother remembered every detail and I also remembered what a wonderful time we'd had. Mary Ann and I had ridden all the rides except the new rollercoaster, the "Comet," which was much higher than the notorious

"Cyclone" that it replaced. Ma had told us we'd have to be a couple of years older to ride the Comet.

Now as she tried to get Pa to understand, her voice shook. "Pa, I enjoyed taking the kids on the trip, but I would have enjoyed it so much more if you had been there with us."

"You're getting excited," Pa yelled. "Slow down—it's not good for you to get excited."

"Pa, every year since we were married, we either didn't have the money to take a vacation, or we couldn't go. You have always spent all of your vacation time either on some work project, or we were broke... Then we couldn't go because of WWII and you were working ten to twelve hours a day six or seven days a week in a defense plant; then it was haying and the farm work in Mumford, or the house needed painting or the garden; it was always something," she said.

"Things are different now; we can get away for a few days. Please, please, this year let's go on a summer vacation!"

Pa's voice was harsh as he replied, "I can see you have been talking to your brother Harold again!"

Pa was not too fond of Uncle Harold, as my uncle was not a man of any status or of any financial importance; just a quiet easygoing man, never in a hurry, who always had time to talk, lived a gentle life and loved people. His favorite pastime was reading travel magazines about everywhere in the world. He enjoyed flowers, nature, and the movies; he loved life and possessions were not very important to him.

Uncle Harold had the unique ability to tell a story enthusiastically describing every scene in vivid detail—and, yes, he had described all of these places above to Ma and me in great detail while Ma and Pa were living with Aunt Viola and Uncle Harold before they purchased the house on

Hinchey Road. I loved the way Uncle Harold always treated me while I was growing up and I cherish all the stories that ·he told!

Ma continued, "Pa, the trim and gutters can wait to be painted later; please let's do something different this year. Let's go on a vacation for a week. Take your pick of the places, or we can go anywhere you say—I don't care where, as long as we have a vacation, some place other than at home!"

Pa turned away and wouldn't look at her.

"I need a change of scenery," she begged. "I want to do something different than take an afternoon ride out past the old farm, or walk by the empty band stand at Charlotte Beach, or drive by the amusement park at Sea Breeze on the lake or stop at Don & Bob's Hot Dog stand. I don't understand why you needed a new car; we never go any place more than thirty miles from Rochester," she said.

"I'm tired of going to the same three different places over and over again. I know the route we are going to take by heart, where we will stop, and how long the ride will be even before we leave home!"

Emphasizing every word as strongly as she could, she told him, "I would just love to have something new to do and look forward to doing it WITH YOU!"

As usual Pa did not listen to her pleas, but remained insensitive to her needs and made no effort to find a way to change the menu of activity. Instead, he did as he pleased, remained home and painted the trim and the gutters on the house during his summer vacation.

I have often thought how things might have been, if only Pa could have been able to listen to Ma with an open mind and attempt to understand. I wished that he could relate in any way to the lyrics of the song "Try a Little Tenderness," written by Irving King. I have wondered... oh, so many times... if things would have been different if Pa had really listened to Ma's pleas not only on this day, but all of the days since 1941, when she had been happy while we were living in an apartment over the A&P grocery store on Lake Avenue.

Shortly after this discussion, Ma returned to her deep depression and thereafter seemed to be making little or no progress for any sustained period of time. After she was released from the hospital on Friday afternoon, she would sometimes ask Pa to take her back to the hospital as early as Friday night or Saturday. This became an ongoing routine.

She might show an interest in life for two or three weeks, and on occasion for several months, but then suddenly she would ask to go back to the hospital and would stay for a month or so, still coming home on some of the weekends. This behavior was never anticipated by me or explained by the doctors; it remained a mystery.

In the meantime, my relationship with my father was unbearable. I blamed Pa totally for Ma's illness and told him so many times. I was sure he was the cruelest man I had ever met.

CHAPTER X

A Whole New World Opens

In 1957, while still living at my parents' home, I joined the Singles Club sponsored by the Diocese of Rochester. The public bus was my only mode of transportation to the first function I attended at St Andrew's Catholic Church on the other side of Rochester. At that dance, I noticed a lovely girl in a stunning orchid-colored dress.

Perry Como's recording of "More Than You Know" was playing as I crossed the floor to where Jeannie was sitting with other girls and asked her to dance. Later, we danced to Bill Doggett's "Honky Tonk."

We danced throughout the evening. Whether the music was fast or slow, Jeannie was a good dancer. Brown-haired, pretty, trim, and well proportioned, she stood about five feet four inches tall and had beautiful big brown eyes. With a warm personality, radiant smile, and soft voice, she was easy to talk to. Jeannie Protchenko had taken the bus from her home on the opposite side of the city, so we parted company at the end of the evening. I thought of her often after that and was excited at the prospect of seeing her again at the next club function.

The next dance was two or three weeks later, but Jeannie was not there. I danced with other girls that evening, but the air had gone out of my balloon. My heart was elsewhere. Jeannie attended the next dance, seeming as excited about seeing me as I was about seeing her again. We talked and danced all evening, became better acquainted, and she gave me her phone number. I was infatuated with her by then, but not having an automobile made dating very difficult. I was more determined than ever to save every dime from my part-time job so I could buy a car.

One May evening, Jeannie and I traveled by bus to see a movie in downtown Rochester. Afterward, while waiting for the bus to take her home, I confided that I was planning to buy an automobile in the near future. Jeannie asked if I had a driver's license. When I explained I needed to buy a car before getting a license, she laughed and said, "You are going to buy a car first?" Then she said, "You are still a boy; I am two years and three months older than you."

Taken aback by her comment, I told her, "I am not a boy, and I will call you after I have my car."

She laughed again, and I decided then that our dating relationship was far too awkward to pursue, as I was paddling upstream against a strong current. If I had any thoughts of our developing a lasting relationship, it would be best not to date her again until I had purchased my car and obtained my license.

In her senior year of high school in 1955 Jeannie had moved to Rochester from New York City with her widowed mother, an immigrant from Russia without employment skills. Sharp and smart, Jeannie worked as a secretary for the Society for the Propagation of the Faith. From her comments, I gathered that her older brothers and sister provided little, if any, financial assistance. Other than a small

Social Security check, Jeannie was her mother's sole financial support. She knew all about tight finances and not having a lot of money to spend on entertainment.

....

While I was looking for my first car, Ma and I were talking one day. She asked, "George, after you get your car would you spend a whole day with me, and take me to some places that I would like to visit? It would be a very special day for me. I have asked Pa, but he always says not today, it's too far."

"Yes, Ma, I will be happy to take you wherever you would like to go, for the whole day, the very first Saturday after I get my driver's license," I said. "You can count on it."

I smiled at her. "Remember, I will be buying my car first, and then I have to learn how to drive before I can take the driving test."

"I understand, and I know you will pass the test on your first try," Ma said. "I will pay for the gas and buy lunch; I would like to leave bright and early, say eight-thirty on Saturday morning, right after breakfast."

"Where will we go?" I asked her.

"I would like to go to Holy Sepulchre Cemetery to visit the baby's grave—your sister Carol, who was stillborn—and my parents' and grandparents' graves and spend a little quiet time there and fix the graves.

"Then I would like us go to St. Michael's Mission—it's high in the hills in Hemlock—and walk through the beautiful Grotto and stop in the old church again at St. Michael's. Maybe the seminarians will be singing like they did when we were there before; they have such lovely voices. And maybe we could also stop in their winery."

She beamed at me. "Do you remember the mission? It's just down the dirt road maybe a mile or so from Uncle Harold's cottage retreat.

"We went to see your Uncle Harold's new place right after it was built in 1949; we went in Uncle Harold's brand new Nash. Uncle George drove because Uncle Harold had not passed his driver's test yet; he was too nervous. You know, he never has been able to pass the driving test, and apparently he is now too old."

As Ma talked about her feelings and what she would like to do on this special day that she was planning, she was smiling and getting excited; and it appeared to me that the old Ma was shining through.

"George, then we could stop for lunch along the way, before we drive to the Trappist Monks' Abbey in Piffard, and while we are there, we can buy a couple loaves of fresh bread in their store; they have the best bread."

"It sounds like a great day," I said.

"Thank you, George—I am looking forward so much to this trip. I have wanted to go to these places for a very long time." She gave me a big smile. "So please don't forget me in all your excitement when you get your driver's license!"

....

I saved every dollar from my part-time job for a down payment for my first car. In May 1957, the part-time job ended, but I had done it! My brother-in-law, Frank, helped me, guiding me through nearly every car lot in Rochester to find that first car. Finally, we found a 1953 Ford, six-cylinder, custom, blue Tudor with a standard transmission. The odometer read only thirty-three thousand miles and the price tag was $895.

With Frank's help I was able to enter a whole new world! He even co-signed the car loan for me at the bank. After I had my car, I pestered him and everyone else I knew to help me to learn to drive. Within three weeks, I had passed the test and looked proudly at my license before tucking it into my wallet.

I fulfilled my promise to Ma the very next Saturday. It was a warm, clear sunny day. After breakfast, we left the house, and our first visit was to Holy Sepulchre Cemetery. Ma told me about how she had saved money from her various part-time jobs and recently she had purchased the marker for the grave of baby Carol, who was born in 1931.

By ten o'clock we were on our way to St. Michael's Mission in Hemlock, we visited the Grotto and the seminarians were singing in church. About two, we stopped for lunch in a restaurant overlooking Conesus Lake, before driving to the Abbey in Piffard, south of Batavia. Ma was in her glory, smiling as she talked about the early years in her marriage and about how broke she and Pa were for so many years during the long Depression, but she said it was also a happy time in her life; she told me many other family stories as we drove along.

It was so good to see Ma so happy! We both had a good time and enjoyed spending the day together; we arrived back home a little after seven p.m. Pa had left a note for us that he went to a restaurant to eat supper.

....

Now there was something I had wanted to do for a long time. I had previously located the address for my high school English teacher, Russell Reed, who had moved to Hamburg, about ninety miles away. The next day, after noon Mass on Sunday, I drove to his house and, when I got out of the car,

Mr. Reed saw me and came out to meet me; he looked very surprised to see me.

I told him that I had looked him up so I could thank him for failing me in English, as that proved to be a real wake-up call for me and a turning point in my life. I told him about going to summer school, reading *Fortitude*, passing English with a grade of ninety-plus, and receiving my diploma. I told him about what I was doing at Dun & Bradstreet and about how happy I was.

Mr. Reed expressed his happiness for me, but I think he might have been a bit fearful when I drove up, perhaps believing I had come to cause him trouble for failing me in English and keeping me from graduating with my class.

....

On Tuesday, I called Jeannie and asked her if she would like to go for a ride the following Saturday. She seemed happy to hear from me and accepted my invitation. We drove to Niagara Falls, Canada, about seventy-five miles away, and spent a lovely day and evening together viewing the falls.

During the next nine months our relationship began to blossom. We had some marvelous times together doing very simple things, including many long drives and many cups of coffee in diners and carhop restaurants. I remember the summer afternoon after a friend installed a used Buick radio in my Ford. The radio was too large to fit behind the dash, so he'd hung a bracket under it. There was a lot of extra wire left over, so you could easily take the radio out of the bracket and put it up on the roof of the car.

We went to Genesee Valley Park, parked the car in the shade by the river, and put the radio on top of the car. Then we spread out a blanket on the grass, kicked back and listened to music, and later danced in the park. This evening was special, and I heard Jeannie, who had a lovely voice, sing a complete song for the first time. It was "When I Fall in Love."

On a Sunday afternoon in mid-October, when the changing leaves were at their peak of color, I picked up Jeannie about one p.m. and asked her if she would like to take a ride to Letchworth State Park, about sixty-five miles south. Known as the "Grand Canyon of the East," it's one of the most scenic areas in the eastern United States. She was very excited with the suggestion, as she had never been there either.

It was a beautiful warm fall day, perfect for a drive, with hardly a cloud in the sky. After I paid the entrance fee to the park, we visited the spectacular gorge and hiked along the trails, marveling at the sheer shale and sandstone cliffs rising five hundred fifty feet, three cascading waterfalls and the high railroad bridge at the upper falls. The gorge, the hills and valleys were ablaze with the leaves' colors, so magnificent and brilliant that the gorge seemed like the kingdom of heaven on earth.

As late afternoon approached, I said, "Jeannie, would you like to stop and get a cup of coffee and a piece of pie or something?"

She said, "Yes, I have not eaten anything since breakfast as I was busy with doing the washing this morning after Mass."

We stopped at the Glen Iris Inn Restaurant, the only restaurant in the park; it was quite small, but stately, perhaps a total of a dozen tables with white tablecloths and fresh flower arrangements on each table. The waitress brought the menu, and to my surprise Jeannie ordered a dinner, and then quickly asked me if it was okay.

I said, "It's fine." When the waitress asked me what I would like, I almost choked at the prices on the menu. I told her, "I would just like a cup of coffee. I had a large lunch." The waitress smiled as she walked away, and shortly brought Jeannie's dinner. It looked wonderful.

A little while later I asked, "Is your dinner okay?" She said, "It's just delicious, George, would you like a taste?"

I told her, "No, I ate a large lunch. I'm not hungry." Had the truth been told, my belly button was rubbing against my backbone. Little did Jeannie know I only had about ten dollars in my pocket; I had not waited for dinner at home to eat Ma's Sunday chicken dinner, as I wanted to be sure to pick Jeannie up on time.

After paying the park entrance fee and the restaurant bill, I only had a dollar and some change left. Phew, I thought, now that was cutting it awful close to being really embarrassed. On the positive side, I learned a lesson that I would never forget.

Before long, we were seeing each other almost every evening, and I was falling head over heels in love with Jeannie.

We were both well aware of each other's concerns about our family situations, and of course about how tight each of our finances were, as we had often discussed both. However, we were always able to put our cares away temporarily and find beauty and happiness in being together; that made it easy to have a positive outlook for the present and for the future.

I had already told Jeannie that I didn't get along with my father and that we were always at odds, and all about my mother and her illness and all the details of her being in and out of the hospital. I had described how nasty Pa could be to me, and that he could be cantankerous for no reason at all.

"Ma is now home from the hospital and seems to be doing pretty good, and I would like to take you to my parents' home to meet them. We wouldn't stay very long," I told Jeannie one day in early March 1958. "Don't be surprised if my father is not very cordial to you; he might be a little cool or grouchy," I warned.

She smiled and said, "Oh, come on, he can't be that bad. He has no reason not to be nice to me."

So on a Sunday afternoon, I took her to meet my parents. I thought, "Oh God, please help me this afternoon—please help Pa treat Jeannie nice." Sadly, that prayer was not going to be answered. Pa was in his normal grumpy mood, and today his nasty streak was in full bloom.

When I introduced him to Jeannie, he grunted, barely acknowledged her presence and went back to reading the newspaper. When he did speak, he talked around her, over her, like she was not there. Peering over his glasses, he looked her over up and down, head to foot, with his beady eyes, sneered, and then went back to his newspaper. He treated Jeannie like garbage.

This horrified Jeannie. I was upset; and now Ma was upset, with her stress showing, and tears forming in her eyes. Ma had just come home about ten days ago, as she was now on trial leave from the New York State Hospital. We quickly said our goodbyes, Pa grunted, we hugged Ma and left.

After we were in the car, I said, "Jeannie, I apologize for my father's behavior. I don't understand why Pa treated you so badly. I'm so sorry. I just can't explain why he can be so nasty for no reason at all." I was unable to offer any explanation of his terrible behavior. "This is not my first experience with Pa's nastiness in the presence of friends of mine; he seems to delight in embarrassing me and making my friends and me feel extremely uncomfortable."

Later, when I confronted Pa about this, he denied any ill treatment of Jeannie, and he laughed. That was Pa's way, denial when confronted. In his eyes, he never was wrong about anything, no matter what he said or did. After he laughed, I became angrier, frustrated, and now aggravated.

Now, I towered over my father, I was almost six feet tall and weighed about one hundred eighty-five pounds; I was as strong as an ox, and street smart. I wanted to hit him so hard with all my strength, but I was fully aware that if I hit him, more than likely I would kill him; and I knew he was not worth it. I also remembered my promise to the sheriff when I was still in high school that I would never again get into a physical brawl with Pa.

I threw up my hands in the air in disgust and left, as it was clearly a waste of time to try to talk with him. Unfortunately, my relationship with Jeannie was never quite the same after that, and things seemed to be increasingly unsettled. Her feelings seemed to be constantly changing, one day she loved me with all of her heart, the next day she was not so sure; one day she was so positive, the next day uncertain; on again, off again.

The future of our relationship seemed to be like a rudderless ship lost at sea. Perhaps she had seen too much of the scope of the problems and attitudes within the Zeller family, as she had more than her share of family problems and financial obligations of her own.

CHAPTER XI

Going West

I had not had an attack of asthma since I left the farm in 1955, but in early 1958 the attacks resurfaced with a vengeance. My asthma continued to be a major problem for me, and I was miserable with my home situation. The doctor suggested that I move to a drier climate, perhaps Denver, Colorado.

In May 1958, with mixed emotions, I gave three weeks notice to my supervisor at D&B and told him of my plans to move to Denver. As I drove out west I continued to question my decision of leaving things up in the air and where I really was in my unsettled on-again-off-again relationship with Jeannie.

After a three-day drive, I arrived in Denver on a Tuesday afternoon and went to the Dun & Bradstreet office early Wednesday morning. I learned that they did not have an opening in Denver, but did have an opening for a correspondent reporter in the small satellite office in Albuquerque, New Mexico. I jumped at the chance and had the opportunity to start on the following Monday.

On Friday afternoon I drove south on Route 285 to Poncha Springs, a town called the Crossroads of the Rockies, and then drove over Poncha Pass and had my first real glimpse of the Rocky Mountains close up, an awesome sight. I continued driving late into the night, then slept a few hours in the car until the break of dawn. The scenery was incredible as the sun rose as I drove down the mountains from above the timberline and into a small town.

It was about six-thirty in the morning; I did not notice any signs as to where I was, and became a little concerned that maybe I had taken a wrong turn in the night, as there were no cars around; I thought...maybe I was in Mexico? What I then saw was a large town square with one-story buildings like the ones I'd seen in Western movies. There were about twenty-five men all dressed in white and wearing sombreros; they were asleep, sitting on the ground leaning up against the sand-colored buildings.

I needed gas, and drove to the outskirts of town, parked in a gas station that was closed for the night and slept in the car until the gas station attendant woke me at about eight a.m. He filled up the car, checked the oil, and washed the windshield. The fourteen gallons of gas at almost 29 cents per gallon totaled $4.05. I commented on the higher price of gas at each of the gas stations since leaving Denver.

He replied, "Gas is always more expensive in the mountains; they have to haul it up here from Albuquerque or from Denver where you came from."

I learned that I was in Taos, New Mexico, just over the Colorado state line and today there was going to be a Memorial Day parade at eleven o'clock. The men that I saw in town were from the Jemez Mountains and were trucked here early this morning be in the parade.

I waited with enthusiasm to see the parade, thinking about the marching bands and the large unit parades I was accustomed to back in Rochester. Finally the parade began, led by the mayor of Taos, riding in the back seat of a Cadillac convertible with apparently the high school beauty queen.

Next came two fire engines and maybe fourteen volunteer firemen; then a group of sixteen or eighteen former military men in uniform marching in step, from each of the four branches of service; then a Boy Scout troop of about ten boys, followed by seven or eight Girl Scouts. They were followed by the twenty-five-member high school marching band playing one of John Philip Sousa's famous marches, and last but not least the twenty-five men marching dressed in the costume of their ancestors from Mexico. That was it; it was over in less than twenty-five minutes including all the delays. I drove on to Albuquerque.

In Albuquerque, a few days later I rented a one-bedroom furnished apartment that was the product of a conversion of a garage, near the University of Mexico; it was conveniently located within ten minutes of the D&B office. About a month later, I celebrated my twentieth birthday, and Jeannie sent me a dozen beautiful long-stemmed red roses, which ignited my troubled emotions. My heart ached for Jeannie. I loved her so; she was constantly on my mind.

In the dry climate, my asthma disappeared as abruptly as it had resurfaced and I felt wonderful. But I missed Jeannie terribly; I thought perhaps sending me the roses was her way as a woman to give me a subtle message of encouragement to continue the pursuit. I really didn't need much encouragement; I was head over heels in love with her—and mostly blind to my health and our financial and family situations when I thought of Jeannie!

So after pondering my emotions for perhaps six or seven weeks I decided to return to Rochester and hopefully develop a lifetime relationship with Jeannie, and my dreams began to grow day by day in anticipation of a wonderful life with her. I gave a three-week notice to my supervisor and told him why I was leaving; he called the reporting manager in D&B's Rochester office in my presence and gave me an excellent review; enabling me to transfer back to my old job.

Upon my return, within minutes of seeing Jeannie I realized that I had completely misread her intentions; the roses were just a gift of friendship to me on my birthday, and nothing more. My continuing efforts to further our relationship romantically were gently rebuffed, and shortly Jeannie ended our relationship permanently. I never really understood why; there never was a clear-cut reason given, never any harsh words spoken between us. Maybe she was just so much stronger and wiser and more mature than I, that she clearly saw insurmountable financial and family problems lying ahead, while all I felt was my love for her, and for the most part I was blind to all the potential problems that might exist for us. Maybe this... Perhaps that...

Periodically, on Sunday I would attend the evening Mass at St. Joseph's Catholic Church; occasionally I would run into Jeannie afterward. She was always alone; we spoke casually, and my heart would pound, but at this juncture I had decided that if this relationship was going to be re-ignited, it was up to Jeannie to openly initiate the relationship. I knew that all she would need to do was squeeze my hand, as my feelings were as strong as ever. But deep in my heart, I knew that would never happen. The lyrics of the song "When I Fall in Love" lingered in my mind; I remembered Jeannie singing it to me on that beautiful· summer afternoon we spent in Genesee Valley Park.

*"When I fall in Love it will be forever
Or I'll never fall in Love
In a restless world like this is
Love has ended before it's begun
And too many moonlight kisses
Seem to cool in the warmth of the sun
When I give my heart it will be completely
Or I'll never give my heart."*

· · · · · · · · · · · ·

About a week after returning to Rochester, I rented a room across town on Cooper Road in Irondequoit, perhaps fourteen miles from my parents' home. The room rent was $10 a week and my elderly landlady took a liking to me and also did my light laundry. Back at my old job at D&B, I gradually redirected my efforts away from my lovelorn feelings by placing most of my attention and time into my job.

About two months later, I got my big break; at twenty years old, I was promoted from a correspondent reporter to a traveling reporter. I covered seven counties on a strict schedule, spending from a week to several weeks in various towns, calling on the businessmen, bankers and accountants, and making visits to the county courthouses. I was gathering information to prepare a Dun & Bradstreet commercial credit report on each business in the town. My income improved quite a bit, and now I also had a little extra expense money in my pocket.

I had much to learn about budgeting my time; early on I was working over sixty hours weekly to be sure my work was completed in a timely manner. The pitfalls of falling behind in the traveling schedule were well known to me, as that had resulted in the failure and termination of several traveling reporters before me; I was determined that I would be successful with this opportunity. Gradually I learned the discipline necessary to succeed and enjoyed the work and its rewards immensely.

············

In the fall of 1960, I moved to Bergen, New York, about thirty miles west of Rochester, and shared a house with Jim Lewis and Dick Talty, two young men who were also reporters at D&B; both were college graduates and they had been living in rooms at the Sheraton Hotel for almost two months.

Jim Lewis, a native of Lincoln, Nebraska, was about twenty-nine years old, stood just over six feet tall, and was well built, with a dark complexion, brown eyes and dark brown hair with a receding hair line. He was a studious, smart, serious young man both in and out of the office; he always was dressed immaculately as if he had just stepped out of Saks Fifth Avenue Men's Store in New York City, with not a hair out of place.

Jim was friendly, but kept his distance. I felt he was destined to rise high in the company as he worked almost every night until nine or ten o'clock; he was a workaholic. He had recently transferred in from the Albany office, where he was a traveling reporter covering several counties located north of Albany to the St. Lawrence River.

Dick Talty was about twenty-three and had transferred in from the Newark, New Jersey, office, as a city reporter. A jolly, heavyset fellow about six feet tall, he was smart as a whip, and a real, regular likeable guy with a great personality and a booming laugh. A prankster at heart, the Irish in him was always evident. We had a lot of fun together for about six months until his father died suddenly that winter and it was necessary for him to return to New Jersey to be near his aging mother, as he was an only child.

We rented this house from Mr. Junior, Sr.—yes, that was really his name—who was abruptly transferred at age sixty-three to the home office in Pittsburgh. As Mr. Junior, Sr., planned to retire in less than two years, he decided that the best thing to do was to rent the house with all the furnishings to someone that he felt would not tear the place up. He did not want to pack up and move all of his things for only a short period of time.

With three bedrooms, two baths, living room, dining room, kitchen, a utility room, and a wood shed, the house was completely furnished with all the appliances, linens, blankets, towels, dishes, glassware, pots and pans. It was right out of an early American furniture magazine. It was decorated to the hilt, complete with antiques and a huge log-burning fireplace with a brick oven and a hook for a large cooking pot. Believe it or not, we broke only one decoration during the year that we lived in the house. Mr. and Mrs. Junior, Sr., were lucky!

CHAPTER XII
Love of a Lifetime

For about five years, my love life was trying. I found myself praying to God, asking him to help me find a girl to love, and for that girl to love me. It seemed like God wasn't listening to my prayers. Year after year passed, and while there were lots of girls, and I fell in love a few times, not one of those girls that I thought I loved felt the same way. However, I didn't give up on the good Lord, and I continued to talk to him.

Then in November 1960, approximately five years after my first conversation with God when I was seventeen, God answered my prayers with a most beautiful girl, and more importantly, a delightful person, simply adorable. She was a real lady with a wonderful attitude and a happy personality that would melt a heart, a joy to be with.

I met this beautiful girl and beautiful person in Katherine (Katie) Buechel on a blind date. Katie was twenty-one years old, about five feet five inches tall, and had long dark brown hair and beautiful brown eyes. She was trim and her one-hundred-fifteen-pound figure was perfect. Katie's lovely complexion glowed, and her smile and laugh radiated;

she looked a lot like Princess Margaret when the Princess was young.

Katie's sister, Mary Ann, worked at Dun & Bradstreet, and she had arranged a blind date for Katie with Dick Talty—who was, some time later, to be my best man at our wedding. Mary Ann fixed me up with a nice girl named Jessica. I'm afraid I had absolutely no interest in Jessica. I spent most of that evening talking to Katie.

A couple of weeks later Mary Ann approached me and, on behalf of Katie, invited me to Katie's office Christmas party at a nice country club. I thought for a minute, wow! I was a little unsure about how it would work out, but then it occurred to me that, in any event, it would be a wonderful meal at Locust Hill Country Club, so I quickly accepted the invitation. I learned later this invitation had been extended to me without Katie's knowledge.

I thought perhaps I should invite Katie out before the Christmas party so that she would be more relaxed with me when we were in the company of her peers. So I asked her to go dancing at the Westminster Inn on the Saturday evening before the Christmas party. The date was really a flop—no better way to say it. Katie had only one drink. She didn't laugh at my jokes, she was extremely quiet, and she wouldn't dance to fast music. Her magical, magnetic attraction had completely disappeared.

Had it not been for the fact that I had accepted her invitation to the Christmas party, I probably would never have called her again. I couldn't help but wonder what had happened to the lovely, happy girl of our first meeting, the one with the exuberant and warm personality. Was she just nervous?

On the evening of the party, I picked up Katie at her home, and we went to the Christmas party at the plush country club. Manhattans were served from a large punch bowl. They were as smooth as silk, and plentiful. Katie was all smiles and introduced me to everyone associated with the prestigious accounting firm of Naramore, Niles and Company.

We sat down to dinner, and Katie asked me whether I would mind if she drank her soup. I replied, "No, if you don't mind if I take off my shoes." As the tables were arranged in a large horseshoe, and everyone would have been able to see my feet, Katie decided to use her soup spoon rather than drink the soup and I kept my shoes on.

The evening turned out to be a lot of fun. We danced, talked, and laughed and Katie's warm, magical personality shone through once again. My interest was very much re-ignited.

I was impressed with the way Katie spoke of her family and the way she made sure to introduce me to her parents and her older brother, Fred. Katie's father, Fred Buechel, about fifty-eight at the time, had a warm smile and a welcoming personality. He was semi-retired, working with his wife in her greenhouse business.

Katie's mother, Olga, was three years younger than Fred, petite and brown-haired. The mother of nine children, she had a big friendly smile and sparkling brown eyes and made me feel very welcome in their home. She had a nice happy laugh that was contagious. I instantly knew these were exceptional people and I looked forward to getting to know them.

Katie was not only a beautiful girl, but also had a wonderful attitude and outlook. I realized that she was everything I had ever dreamed of and much more, a girl with a warm, outgoing personality that would melt your heart away. I knew that Katie was the girl for me. It was only a short time later that I realized that she loved me too, and we decided we wanted to announce our engagement and marry the following October.

In later years, I began to understand why it took God so long to answer my prayers: This girl was still in the making for me, and God was keeping her on hold for me, but probably most of all, the good Lord was waiting for me to grow up.

For the most part, I was still living from paycheck to paycheck, and my savings were a little short to buy a nice engagement ring. It was not until the spring of 1961, when I received my income tax refund check, that I could afford to buy the diamond ring. I gave Katie the ring in St. Jerome's Catholic Church in East Rochester, and I asked Jesus for his help to keep our love at least as strong as it was on that day for the rest of our lives.

After Katie and I were officially engaged, I went to see my parents. I told them about my engagement, and that I wanted to bring Katie to meet them. My mother was very happy and excited for me; she suggested that I bring her to dinner. Later, I pulled Pa aside in the back yard and told him that if he did not treat Katie cordially and with respect, I would guarantee him that he would physically regret his actions. I told him that I loved Katie very much and would never allow him to hurt her in any way, as he had hurt Jeannie a few years ago.

Pa was nice at the dinner, rather quiet, but friendly. Ma was thrilled to meet Katie and made her feel welcome. There was no stress showing on Ma's part whatsoever. She was warm, kind to Katie, and prepared a delicious chicken dinner.

I remember taking Katie a short time later to visit my mother, who was back in the New York State Mental

Hospital, where she shared a ward with at least twenty other women. Ma was extremely depressed; she was having a bad day. Katie was compassionate, demonstrating deep understanding and maturity. The situation was difficult for her but she showed no stress, just compassion.

Ma's mental health continued on a rollercoaster, showing some improvement at times and then a downturn into depression. Ma made several more trips to the emergency room as a result of failed attempts to commit suicide.

....

In April 1961, Katie's sister Mary Ann was getting married, and Katie was in the wedding party. After the wedding rehearsal, we all went back to the Buechel homestead for drinks and something to eat.

During the course of the evening, Katie's dad asked me, "George, do you know of the McCombs family in Mumford?"

I said, "Yes, they are my second cousins; they live on Armstrong Road in Mumford, the same road that I grew up on."

Fred replied, "Isabelle McCombs is my second cousin by way of the Schmitt family, and my mother's maiden name was Anna Schmitt." So, I thought, I must be related to Katie's father somehow.

Oh no, I thought, would Katie and I still be allowed to marry? She and I contacted Father Hempel at St. Jerome's Catholic Church to acknowledge the facts and ask for his help. Father Hempel told us the Catholic Church would require a family tree to show the ancestry of the family, showing the connection between Katie's dad and me. This was at first quite alarming. We feared that it might prevent our marriage.

The genealogy research went slowly and included several visits on weekends to different relatives, and later to Holy Ghost and Holy Sepulchre Cemeteries to gather the necessary information to prepare the family trees. It turned out that Katie's grandmother, Anna Schmitt Buechel, and my grandfather, George Schmitt, were brother and sister, and that made Katie and me second cousins, which proved to be acceptable in the eyes of the church.

In July, my traveling schedule at D&B had me working in the southern tier of New York State about one hundred miles from Rochester; therefore I was going to be out of town on my mother's birthday, an important day to her. Previously I had asked Katie, my wife to be, if she would take a gift to my mother on her birthday on the 31st. Katie said she would be happy to take care of it, as she knew how important it was to me.

On the 31st of the month, after work Katie, accompanied by three members in her car pool, drove the ten miles west of Rochester in rush hour traffic to deliver my gift. When Ma opened the door, Katie said, "Happy birthday! George wanted me to deliver this gift to you."

Ma replied, "Katie, it's not my birthday today, you're a month early; my birthday is August 31." Then Ma roared with laughter!

When I called that evening, Katie told me about my error on the date of Ma's birthday, and said, "George, while it was not your mother's birthday today, the surprise was the best gift you could have given her. She was tickled pink!"

Katie and I married in October 1961, with Father Hempel officiating in St. Jerome's Catholic Church. It was a large church wedding, and the bride was beautiful in her white wedding gown and train. She was the last of the five daughters in the Buechel family to marry, and the event occurred in the finest of Buechel tradition.

After the wedding ceremony was over, a sit-down dinner at noon was served at the Country House Restaurant and Party House for the wedding party, the immediate family, and the aunts and uncles, totaling approximately one hundred people. An evening reception at St. Nicholas Hall was held for about three hundred guests. It was complete with a full buffet, open bar, and a six-piece dance band.

My father ate and left shortly thereafter, before the music began, stating that he needed to go home so he could get a good night's sleep, as he was to be at work by six a.m. This left Ma very upset, but she didn't show it. It also left her without a dancing partner for the photo of the family wedding dance. This problem was solved when a young married friend of the family who recognized the dilemma asked Ma to dance with him.

．．．．．．．．．．．．

Before Katie and I were married we planned to move out west to Phoenix, Arizona, to insure that my asthma would not be a future problem for us. Katie's parents suggested that we live with them, as it did not make any sense to rent an apartment for such a short time before moving out west, so we lived with them and paid room and board until the following August, when we drove out to Phoenix.

Katie was now pregnant with our first child, and shortly after we arrived in Phoenix, we discovered that the heat did not have a positive effect on Katie. The doctor suggested that we needed a cooler climate; within a month we moved back to East Rochester. Katie's parents welcomed us home and invited us to live with them as they had plenty of room, and we did get along just fine.

We accepted their kindness and lived with Fred and Olga for seven years until we bought our home on Wickford Way in Fairport, two miles away. We kept things straight up and paid our way, paying room and board weekly, increasing the amount as our children arrived and the cost of living increased.

••••••••••••

In mid-1962, I left Dun & Bradstreet and joined Lincoln Rochester Trust Company. Our first child, John, was born that November, and finances were tight. In March 1963, Katie was given the opportunity to go back to work for the tax season at her old accounting firm, Naramore & Niles. She jumped at the opportunity to earn additional income; however, the babysitting situation needed to be resolved.

Ma was doing fine at the time, so we approached her about taking care of John while Katie worked the income tax season. Ma was excited and quickly agreed, as this was her first opportunity to babysit a grandchild, and this was her tenth grandchild. It was also a chance for Ma to earn some spending money.

We would leave home each work day morning by six-forty-five to take the baby across town to Chili, about twenty miles away on the west side of Rochester, during the rush hour traffic, to my parents' place on Hinchey Road. Then we drove ten miles in rush hour to work; after work we would pick up John and return home about six-thirty in the evening.

Even though this was a labor of love for Ma, this resulted in a real strain on her as it totaled more than ten hours daily. It proved to be way too many hours each day and far too confining for Ma; it also was too great a distance for us to travel during the peak traffic rush hours each day. So shortly thereafter we made other babysitting arrangements for John with a lady living nearby.

Later, Katie's mother, Olga, said she would like to take care of John as her busy season was over in her greenhouse business and she would have plenty of time. While she did not want to accept payment for babysitting, we insisted and paid her the same as we had paid my mother and the lady up the street.

Katie, now pregnant with our second child, continued working with Naramore, Niles & Co. until shortly before the birth of our daughter, Katherine, in late October 1963.

In the meantime, Ma had entered a new world, and was excited and aware that she could earn a fair amount of spending money. Periodically she would find work cleaning houses like she did before moving to Mumford in 1947; she did some babysitting, and occasionally she cared for elderly people for four to eight hours at a time.

Some time later she answered an ad in the newspaper and found what she considered a dream job. This job had a convenient time schedule, ten a.m. to two p.m., and only three days per week, just a four-hour babysitting job for Miss Rita's children at Miss Rita's home, which was just a short bus ride away. Miss Rita was something of a celebrity on the local TV scene, with a children's show being broadcast five days per week Ma enjoyed the novelty of being associated with her, and was paid handsomely. She seemed happy for quite a while doing this job; then like in the past a pattern developed... Ma would get bored with a job and decide to quit.

Since Pa had always turned down all of her requests to take a trip away from home even for only a few days, she knew it would serve no purpose to discuss her plans; it would only result in being turned down again. Sometimes she would suddenly take a vacation by bus for several days, seldom for longer than five to ten days. She would always send us a postcard from the city where she was staying.

Over the ensuing years when Ma was doing fine at home and not depressed, she would often find a part-time job through the newspaper ads, work for awhile and save her money, keeping it in her own bank account. Then without notice to anyone she would suddenly go off traveling on a bus by herself while Pa was at work.

She would leave Pa a note on the kitchen table saying she was going to take a trip for several days and she would be home after a while. When she returned home she would call me on the telephone; she would always be happy and tell me all about her trip. But then abruptly Ma's depression would return and she would return to the hospital for a while and then the cycle would start all over.

In January 1964, Katie took over the flower business, Peacock Flower Farm, from her retiring parents and rented the facilities. On Good Friday evening in 1964, Pa and Ma came to visit at the flower farm. Entering the showroom greenhouse, which had a large variety of Easter plants on display, Pa opened the conversation by commenting, "Oh my, look at all these flowers and plants; it's forecasted for a snowy weekend and bad weather for this Easter."

As he walked through the greenhouses, he went on and on, "Look at all this inventory... Oh, my God," pointing out how many plants we had, shaking his head, noting the amount of flowers in each of the five greenhouses, as well as the garage full of cut flowers in buckets of water.

Finally, I had heard enough. "Pa, if that is the purpose of your visit—to agitate—you can leave now, as we do not need to listen to your worrisome comments. We are very well aware of the current unfavorable weather forecasted for this Easter weekend, and we don't need any more pressure than we have."

Pa and Ma left shortly thereafter. Privately, Katie confided that she was very upset with me because of the manner in which I had spoken to my father. The weather for Easter weekend turned out to be much milder than was forecasted, and Katie's first major holiday was a big success and we sold out to the bare walls.

....

Later in 1964, when Pa had his annual physical at work, the x-ray of the lungs revealed that one of his lungs had spots on it, which proved to be cancerous. Within a week they operated and removed a cancer the size of a grapefruit and one lung, along with part of his vocal cords.

It was a six-hour operation at St. Mary's Hospital. When the doctor came out and told us what he had removed and that Pa was very weak, I asked, "Doctor, what are Pa's chances?"

He replied, "Fifty-fifty."

After about ten days in the hospital Pa was released and came home. We bought him a recliner so he could recline, as he was not allowed to lie flat. He had to blow often through a long tube to keep his lung clear and aid in recovery.

When I took Pa to the doctor for his follow-up visit, privately I asked, "Doctor, how is my father doing?"

He said, "George, I've never seen a man so determined to live and he is recovering at a phenomenal rate."

Within three months Pa was allowed to go back to work; however, he was limited as to the amount of weight he could lift and was no longer allowed to repair the pumps at Gerber Baby Foods. Instead he was given a job in the tool and parts room. Pa did not like the confinement of being eight hours in the tool room; he retired about three months later.

During Pa's recovery, I remember Ma expressing herself privately to me. She was deeply depressed and struggling terribly at the time. She said with great anxiety, yet with absolutely no compassion or emotion, "George, Pa stayed by me while I was having my problems all these years; and I will do the same for him. It's my duty to take care of him until he recovers."

. . . .

At Lincoln Rochester Trust Company I had progressed gradually up the ranks from starting as a collector, a mandatory prerequisite to lending. Now in early summer of 1966, I was using some of my financial background from D&B in performing comprehensive analytical reviews of automobile dealerships and writing and making loan review presentations.

One day at lunch time I had left the office in Midtown Plaza and had just walked across Main Street; I was deep in thought and in a hurry to go to lunch before an appointment with an accountant a couple of blocks away. Lo and behold, there was Jeannie smiling and standing right in front of me by Sibley's Department Store; my heart raced uncontrollably in excitement for a moment. She gave me a big hug and we talked for a few minutes; in the course of the small talk she told me little had changed in her life and she was still single. She appeared very interested in what I was doing, my marriage and hearing about my children, and asked a lot of general questions.

My last contact with Jeannie had been nearly eight years ago. This sudden emotional encounter with the past unnerved me for a split second, but these feelings passed as quickly as they had appeared. My thoughts quickly turned to my happiness and my successful marriage to my loving wife Katie and our young family. This love story of yesterday was placed back on the shelf with all the other memories of my life.

....

When I got home from the office on a Thursday night that summer, there was a postcard in the mail from Ma. It was headlined *From Bangor, Maine, "The Home of the Lobster Roll,"* and showed a water scene with lobster pots.

Ma's message on the card read, "Hi, George and Katie, I am having a great time on vacation, have been traveling for almost a week. I was on Cape Cod for a couple of days. The weather is nice here in Bangor; but I am running out of money, please send me $200, so I can pay the motel bill and buy a bus ticket home. I will pay you back when I get home. Love, Ma."

Below that was a line saying, "P.S. DON'T TELL PA."

There was no name of the motel, address, or a telephone number on the postcard postmarked from Bangor, Maine! Well, I thought, here it is Thursday night about six o'clock; how am I ever going to find where Ma is staying in Bangor? While I ate supper, I pondered the situation and realized the only place that I could think of to ask for help was the local police department there.

I called the Bangor Police Department and they gave me a desk sergeant; I told him my story and he quietly chuckled, and then asked me several questions. "When was the postcard dated? What kind of car is she driving? Give me a description of her and her personality... How old is she, how tall, is she thin or chubby, what color are her eyes and hair... long hair or short hair? Does she wear glasses, does she smoke or drink? Was she well dressed, did she often travel, was she accustomed to the finer things in life?"

I emphasized to him that Ma was traveling by bus, and was a very friendly, gentle lady who had been frugal all of her life. "She loves to go to Mass every day and loves to sit by the water," I said, "and more than likely would choose an inexpensive but clean motel in or close to town, near a Catholic church and a restaurant, and not too far from the water."

The desk sergeant was gentle as he spoke, "Sir, let me assure you that Bangor, Maine, is a relatively small and safe place. I think we will be able to locate your mother this evening; there is no need to worry. We will call you as soon as we locate her." I thanked him, gave him our telephone number and address, and hoped I would hear from him by noon on Friday so that I could wire Ma the money she needed.

I said to Katie, "If Pa calls looking for Ma, I will have to tell him what is going on, but only if he calls."

It wasn't two hours later that the sergeant called, and said, "I have found your mother, and I went to see her; I talked with her at the motel. She is fine and happy, and not the least bit concerned."

The sergeant continued, "When I asked her why she didn't write on the card where she was staying, she replied, 'I must have forgotten; but my son George said he can find anyone, anywhere... whatever that means!'"

I explained to the sergeant, "A few years ago during my career at the bank I had worked for awhile doing skip tracing on serious delinquent accounts. Apparently, I had told Ma what I was doing in the bank at the time; and she took that to heart."

He laughed and gave me the name, address and telephone number of the motel in Bangor and the room number where Ma was staying. I thanked him for all of his help, and he replied he was glad that everything was okay. Then I called Ma, who was happy to hear from me, but totally unconcerned, and reiterated what she had told the sergeant. I wired the money to her Friday morning through Western Union.

Ma called about four days later to say she was home. Katie, the kids and I drove over that evening to see her. She was glad to be home and happy to see us, and began to tell us all about where she had been and all that she had experienced and of course about the new foods, like lobster rolls, that she had eaten on her trip. Pa was not interested in hearing about Ma's adventures and went outside in the back yard.

CHAPTER XIII

Tragedy

From the wonderful high that Ma was experiencing within when she returned from her trip to Bangor, it was barely a month until she returned to a deep state of depression. Again she failed in another attempt to end her life with an overdose of medicine. Once again Pa found her unconscious in bed at home when he came home from work. The empty bottle of her depression pills and a water glass were on the nightstand; this was perhaps the fifth or sixth time this event had occurred.

She was taken by ambulance to Strong Memorial Hospital and remained there a few days before being transferred back to the New York State Hospital. After a month or so the previously established routine returned, and Ma was allowed to go home on weekends at first, then for five days and gradually staying home for longer periods.

This time things were a little different; she never again showed outward interest in finding a part-time job or pursuing another bus trip; she never again spoke about going on a summer vacation. Her beautiful warm eyes now were always glassy. Her familiar gentle smile, her loving peaceful touch and warm personality were gone; locked up within, replaced with an inner emptiness for months on end.

Any improvement in Ma's condition would be temporary and short lived; then as in the past she would often drift again into a quiet deep depression for days on end. Sometimes she would resurface gradually for a day or two, a week or longer, and then this cycle of depression in her life would return over and over again.

. . . .

Twelve years after Ma's first attempt to commit suicide by taking an overdose of sleeping pills while living on the farm in Mumford, she succeeded in taking her life. This time her effort took place next to the garage at my parents' home on Hinchey Road, where she poured gasoline from the lawn mower gas can over herself and set herself on fire.

Burned over eighty percent of her body, Ma died an agonizing death three days later in May 1967, in Strong Memorial Hospital in Rochester, completing a full circle since her first trip there in 1955. Ma's body was disfigured so badly by the burns that it was necessary to have a closed casket for the wake at the funeral home; we placed Ma's picture on top of the casket.

CHAPTER XIV
Life Continues

Two years later Pa announced that he had sold the house on Hinchey Road and had purchased a mobile home, completely furnished, near York, some ten miles southwest of Mumford.

"What are you going to do with the furniture—in particular, the reclining chair that I gave you to help you with your convalescence after your surgery for cancer?" I asked him.

Pa replied, "I'm giving almost everything to my brother Donald; he recently remarried and can use it."

"I want the green reclining chair if you no longer want it," I said.

"Then you better come and get it," he told me. "Donald is coming to get the furniture soon."

I picked up the chair that evening and also took Ma's upholstered rocker. Those two chairs turned out to be my inheritance. Not even the boxes of family photographs or Ma's recipes were passed down to Pa's children. I was sure glad I had taken a few family pictures from the cardboard box in the attic when I moved out of the house in 1958, or I would have none today.

....

One Christmas Day, a year or so later, Pa called to say he had nowhere to go for Christmas dinner. That brought back memories of my own experience in 1959, alone on Christmas when I lived in a room on Cooper Road in Irondequoit. Not a single family member had called me during the day. So about four-thirty in the afternoon I went for dinner alone at the Maplewood Diner on Ridge Road. I had never felt so alone in my life as I did on that Christmas Day. I shared the holiday with the short-order cook and one old man at the other end of the counter. It was so eerily quiet in that diner, you could have heard a pin drop.

On this particular Christmas, when Pa called, Katie was sick with the flu. She was exhausted. She had not had a day away from the business in over eight weeks. Still, we invited Pa for Christmas dinner. Unannounced, he brought his brother, Uncle Harold Zeller, with him. Pa's opening comment was not "Merry Christmas" but "You know what you ought to do..."

I cut him off several times, but he insisted on starting all over again with his unsolicited advice.

Finally I told him, "Pa, if you have come to visit my family and me and to share this Christmas Day, you are welcome. You are welcome to share our Christmas dinner and drink and enjoy the warmth of our home and our hospitality. However, Pa, if you've come to see what we have or don't have, or to tell us how to live our lives, you can leave now!" He finally got the message.

Some time later I discovered that Pa had actually been invited to my brother Walter's home for Christmas dinner, and had canceled. I suspect he canceled because he learned that his brother Harold was alone, and he had reservations about taking his brother to Walter's, since Walter had seven children at the table.

Three years after Ma's death, Pa met a lady named Lillian Moody, about sixty years old; she had been married briefly and divorced many years ago, and had no children. Lillian had blond hair worn in a French twist; she had blue eyes and a fair complexion, and dressed nicely. She had recently retired from the Rochester Telephone Company where she had worked for twenty-nine years.

Lillian was six years younger than Pa; after dating about a year they decided to get married in 1971. Lillian agreed to marry Pa with one condition: that they move to south Florida immediately after they were married before setting up housekeeping, and Pa agreed.

Pa did not invite his children to the wedding. He invited his brothers as representatives of his family. I believe that he was afraid that his children would put a damper on his wedding day with Lillian, so, in Pa's true form, he denied his children again.

Lillian had a warm smile and pleasant way about her, nonconfrontational, without any opinion on anything; she always was agreeable about anything with anyone and just went with the flow. She was very secretive about her family and her past. Her disposition enabled her to heap mounds of flattery, adulation and blarney upon everyone, and Pa was in his glory with all of her attention. She was quite laid back and had an uninvolved, congenial personality; cooking and entertaining were not her forte.

She was definitely not the grandmother type and completely avoided this role, even though Pa had thirteen grandchildren ranging in age from five up to fifteen. In this regard she was similar in nature to my father, as Pa never enjoyed his grandchildren. He didn't have it in him to find the interest, to take the time to find a way to reach out to love, to express love, to take the time to share, to show warmth, to talk with his grandchildren or allow his grandchildren to love him.

Pa was still like stone, no different in this role as a grandfather than he had been as the father with his own children. He was still all about him and his life; nothing had changed, no lesson had been learned from all of the heartache and agony of the past. Once again Pa passed the opportunity to reach out, feel and express love to, and be loved by all of his grandchildren.

. . . .

While on vacation in Florida in the winter of 1975, Katie and I took our children, John and Katherine, then almost teenagers, to visit their Grandpa Zeller and Lillian at their condo in Deerfield Beach. Katie was visiting with Lillian while Pa, John, Katherine, and I played shuffleboard. Pa was very aggressive, and I caught him trying to cheat the children several times.

Again, when they played rummy that evening, he was caught several times trying to cheat. The children complained that Grandpa was cheating. Pa was very serious, though. He was going to win regardless of who he was going to take advantage of. While it was a different form or style, it was still the same old ways of Pa that I had experienced during my youth on the farm. It upset Katie and me and our children, and we never allowed our children to participate in games with their Grandpa Zeller again.

From all appearances and comments, Lillian and Pa seemed very happy with each other. They frequented several different restaurants in the Pompano Beach and Deerfield Beach area, and they drove more than two hundred fifty miles one way, a couple of times, across Florida to New Port Richey to visit Pa's sister, Laura, and her husband, Milo Chase.

Together they briefly visited Katie and me and our children at our home after we moved to St. Petersburg, Florida. They drove north several times in the summer to visit Pa's relatives and Lillian's friends in the Rochester area, and in later years Pa even rode on an airplane for the first time to go north for vacation in the summer. Reluctantly, I could not help but notice that Lillian was showered with all of the things that Ma pleaded for and was denied for so many years.

George Zeller with Lillian and Walter Zeller, 1975

Pa and Lillian always appeared to be happy with each other throughout their fourteen years of marriage until my father's death in 1985 at the age of eighty-two. Lillian's manner never varied during the next twenty-one years until her death at age ninety-six in 2006.

....

I am so thankful that our children had the opportunity to grow up experiencing the kindness and love of their Grandpa and Grandma Buechel. I found a father image and mentor in my father-in-law, Fred Buechel, that I had never experienced with my father, and I grew to love him.

He was a great teacher—patient, loving and full of encouragement and trust. Fred was a hard worker and expected the same from others. From him I learned that it's easy to outperform your expectations when you are given encouragement and trust.

I also loved my mother-in-law, Olga Buechel. She was kind, patient, and loving. She always had a smile, and she made me feel glad to be around her. My wife's parents were very supportive of me, accepting me and making me feel they were proud to have me as their son-in-law.

When Fred and Olga died, I cried and grieved deeply. I truly had lost real family and wonderful friends.

John and Grandpa Buechel, Christmas 1963

Olga (Grandma Buechel) 1967. Below, Katherine Ann and Grandma Buechel, February 1964

John on tractor with Grandpa Buechel, Spring 1969.

· · · · · · · · · · · ·

Unfortunately, I cannot say that of my father. However, I can say that I never missed a meal, was cold or was physically abused by my father. I loved my mother dearly. I remember her as a kind, gentle, and loving person with a warm smile.

Ma said, "It is up to you to be considerate of others and to take responsibility for your own life." She told me that all the choices in life are yours to make, and the consequences of your choices are yours to bear, so measure the board three times before you cut it, because lumber is expensive. In making decisions, it is important to consider what the effects of your decisions will be on others, as this is also your responsibility.

"Remember," she said, "if you don't listen, you will surely feel."

My mother often told the story about a young man in jail who asked for his mother. His mother came. They spoke for a few minutes and then her son asked her to come closer as he wanted to whisper something to her. She moved closer and leaned her head against the jail cell bars, and her son took a deep breath and sighed, then leaned close to his mother's ear and bit her ear off. His mother jumped away in agony, demanding to know why he had done that. He replied, "Because you didn't make me listen."

Ma went on to say, "George, I never want you to bite my ear off, so I'm going to be sure that you listen."

Growing up, I had for years watched Ma practice her faith, reaching out to help the less fortunate, sometimes bearing Pa's criticism for her generosity.

•••••••••••

After eleven years at Lincoln Rochester Trust Company, in 1973 I was promoted to an officer at the bank. I continued my employment at Lincoln, and Katie continued successfully operating the Peacock Flower Farm until the end of 1978, when we decided to relocate to St. Petersburg, Florida, so that we could enjoy the warmer weather and sail our Columbia 8.7 sailboat year round.

In January 1979, I joined SunTrust Bank in Tampa, Florida, and we moved to St. Petersburg, across Tampa Bay.

CHAPTER XV

Reuniting with My Brother

In the late summer of 1996, Katie and I shared a long weekend with my sister, Mary Ann, and her husband, Frank, while at a Dept. 56er's convention in Greenville, South Carolina. Mary Ann, then sixty-one years old, told me that she had got nothing at all from home when Pa sold the house on Hinchey Road.

This was the first time I had seen Mary Ann since our daughter's wedding in 1990, and it was her first time away from her home in Norcross, Georgia, since she'd suffered a major stroke in mid-March of 1996. While reminiscing, Mary Ann and I shared our concerns for our brother, Walter, who continued to recall troublesome memories of Pa during his youth on the farm in Mumford.

I visited Rochester in July 1996, to attend my forty-first class reunion. While in Rochester, I visited Walter, then sixty-six. Together we visited Mumford, where we had grown up, as well as Caledonia High School and the surrounding area. We talked at great length about our youth. Eventually, Walter's pent-up feelings gushed out like water through a break in a dam as he related stories of his teenage years and his unrelenting hostility toward Pa.

I listened to Walter as he told one story after another about his encounters with Pa on the farm. He also talked about Pa's sale of the house on Hinchey Road in 1969. He described with disgust the opportunity Pa gave him to buy the old gas mower for $50. Pa had purchased the lawn mower new in 1952, while living on the farm in Mumford. Walter was furious at the exorbitant price his own father had demanded for a seventeen-year-old lawn mower. Walter paid Pa the $50.for the mower, but grumbled about it for years.

Even after forty-two years of marriage, raising seven children and shepherding them through college, Walter was haunted by his bitter memories. I tried to demonstrate patience and kindness with Walter. I felt mounds of compassion for my brother, but I could not make him understand that he was not alone.

Walter told me he still drove out to Mumford and stopped at the farm on Armstrong Road on a regular basis, and that he just couldn't shake the past no matter how hard he tried. I tried to console him and share with him my own attempts to deal with the memories of my youth. But Walter would not listen; he interrupted me continually and took over the conversation, telling of his own hurt feelings and painful experiences. Eventually I realized that Walter was unwilling or unable to contain himself and share the conversation.

When Walter and I drove by and stopped at the farm in the summer of 1996, the fields along the road had not been worked in more than forty years and were overgrown and had returned to the wild, probably much like they were in 1945 when our family moved to Mumford.

The old farm buildings as they looked in 1997.

As Walter gazed out at the field by the barn, I said to him, "Walter, I want to stop in and say hello to Mrs. Livermore across the street—would you like to join me?" He said, "No, I stopped by a couple of weeks ago."

I went to the house, where her daughter Maureen recognized me and opened the door. She smiled and pointed to the kitchen, where her mom was sitting. At first Mrs. Livermore, now eighty-nine years old, didn't recognize me, but as soon as I said, "You used to give me fresh baked sugar cookies," she called me by name, smiled and was very happy that I had stopped by. Their house was just the same as I remembered it from more than forty years ago.

Subsequently, I decided to write a letter to my brother. In it, I would share my knowledge and some of my experiences with him; so perhaps he could really understand that he was not alone.

August 19, 1996

My Dear Brother Walter,

It was great to see you again after all those years. How wonderful it was to spend some leisurely time with you and to reminisce and see some of the old places. It was like some of the old times of our youth, of days gone by.

Walter, I have been thinking a great deal about you as I walk along the beach, and am concerned about your continuing negative feelings of our father during your teenage years. I do understand your feelings.

Yes, Walter, it is true that Pa never came to see you play baseball, particularly in 1948, your senior year and the year Caledonia won the championship and you went on to play in the Briggs Stadium in Detroit, Michigan. It was he who missed the thrill. Yes, it is true that he never saw me play tennis. But the saddest fact is that he didn't support our sister Mary Ann, who had the brains and high marks in chemistry, math, history, and Latin, and the desire to go to college to study to be a Registered Nurse.

It is also true that our Pa worked the B shift, 3:30 P.M. to midnight, as far back as I can remember, except for my senior year 1954-1955….

(This letter is continued later in the book.)

CHAPTER XVI

Forgiving Pa

Throughout the twelve years of Ma's illness, I bitterly and adamantly blamed Pa for her suffering and, ultimately, for her death. I never stopped telling Pa how I felt. I fervently believed that his unremitting harsh treatment of Ma over the years was the cause of her mental illness. I had nothing but contempt for Pa.

In the late 1960s, I forgave Pa for his nastiness to me. I now believe that Pa was a very insecure person who was unable to love himself. I couldn't recall ever seeing him express joy for someone else who had good fortune; it seemed he could be happy only for his own good fortune.

I couldn't recollect any kind words or praise or even words of encouragement ever from Pa for his immediate family—never a "well-done" or "thank you" or "I appreciate your help," or "You sure have worked hard," or a congratulations on a promotion. I never saw or received a gentle, comforting touch or heard a comforting word from him. I do remember, though, that Pa was always looking for compliments for himself. He never missed a chance to tell me how good he was.

I forgave Pa a long time ago, just as I had stopped seeking his love or approval when I saw it no longer had any value to me. I realized many years ago that, in my marriage to Katie, I loved more, and was more deeply loved, than I had ever dreamed possible. I received love daily from my children, and I had the acceptance of my family. This feeling, I knew then, could not be bought or sold; it was mine as long as I treasured it and nurtured it.

I began to see that I was a very wealthy man and a pretty good fellow too. At that point in my life, I began to feel pity for my father because of all the beautiful and tender experiences of life he had cheated himself out of.

....

Long ago, when I was seventeen years old in my first year on the job at D&B, I had met a successful analytical reporter, Peter Anderson. In his mid-forties, he was married with four children. He was a gentleman, stately and dignified in manner.

Somehow he recognized my silent anguish and, unbeknown to me, contacted a doctor who was a friend of his. The doctor in turn made the clinic services of Strong Memorial Hospital available and offered them to me. I went to the clinic in the hospital for an extensive physical at a total cost of approximately $30. This physical was done and payment was made over a three- or four-month period with numerous doctors examining me, although I always spoke with only one doctor.

In the course of time, we discussed Ma's health in great detail. Based on those conversations, the doctor arranged for me to speak with a psychiatrist. I met regularly, sometimes twice or three times a week, with the psychiatrist for one-hour sessions, sometimes longer, for six to eight months. I was charged minimally, about $2 or $3 each week, no matter the number of visits.

As a result of these visits, I finally came to some important realizations: Ma and Pa were good people. They worked hard, paid their bills and really wanted the best for their family. We never missed a meal; we were never cold or physically abused. However, my parents never displayed any fondness or affection for each other in my presence. I never saw any hugs between the two, much less a kiss.

I don't recall Pa or Ma praising or complimenting each other. I remember Ma complaining about how little money he earned, and Pa complaining about how much money she spent. It's a shame that, when they married, they didn't leave their families and cling to each other and support and truly love and enjoy each other.

From Pa and Ma I learned to work hard, not to quit, standing up for what I believed, to persevere. From Ma I learned to work smart, to listen and question, and to make my own decisions based on facts. From both of them I learned honesty and integrity. Ma taught me to be flexible and self-sufficient, to dream, to care, and to love with all my heart. She also taught me about the love of Jesus, and to keep him close to my heart, as Jesus would always be there for me. "Remember to talk to Jesus; don't be a stranger," she often told me.

· · · · · · · · · · · ·

A long time later, after many years of wrongfully blaming Pa for Ma's illness I came to a new understanding based on my own wife's experience. In about 1992, Katie, who had always been an extremely happy person, began experiencing serious symptoms of crying, argumentativeness, sleeplessness, depression, sweating and chills, nervousness, and general feelings of not being in control.

I saw in Katie's eyes the same glassiness and that forlorn look that I had seen in my mother's eyes when I helped her out of the creek so many years ago. My mind was ravaged with the painful memories of my mother. I feared for Katie and myself. I felt totally helpless to guide her, so I asked her to make an appointment with her physician.

After Katie told her doctor of her symptoms, she also told him about her mother-in-law's lengthy mental illness and that she had committed suicide after being in and out of the New York State Mental Hospital for twelve years.

The doctor told Katie that his own mother had suffered from the serious effects of menopause and spent many years of her life in a state mental institution, many years before menopause was understood. He explained that millions of women across the United States had been thought to be mentally ill and had been locked up in state institutions; some were even treated with electrical shock.

The doctor prescribed estrogen and progesterone for Katie, and a few days later she was her old happy self again. Katie told me about her conversation with her gynecologist. Shortly thereafter, when I had an appointment with my own doctor, I asked him about menopause and told him about Katie's conversation with her physician and about Ma having committed suicide.

My doctor told me his mother also suffered from the effects of menopause and had committed suicide, and he confirmed Katie's doctor's information. I believe wholeheartedly that Ma suffered from the devastating effects of severe menopause, not from mental illness. Today, menopause is treated routinely with drugs that simulate estrogen and progesterone. Treatment has been dramatically improved since 1955, but more still needs to be done, especially for the underprivileged women and the education of men.

I am also very aware that Pa could have abandoned Ma in the New York State Hospital, as many men did in that situation. Pa was only about fifty-two years old at the time; it is impossible to imagine what he experienced during her declining twelve years. His anguish must have been unbearable, knowing that his children—and in particular I myself, who had openly and repeatedly blamed him for years—and Ma's family, the Schmitts, all held him accountable for Ma's problem.

In 1985 Pa died, not knowing that Ma had suffered and died from the terrible effects of menopause and that she was not mentally ill. He never knew that he was not in any way responsible for her death.

CHAPTER XVII

Closure Found in the Family Tree

In the fall of 1997, I decided to join Katie, who had been working on her family tree. Since we are second cousins, we share a greater than normal interest in this project. Katie's grandmother was Anna Schmitt, the sister of George J Schmitt, Sr., my grandfather.

I began to work on the Schmitt side of the family. By early December, I was well under way and had contacted all of the Schmitt cousins. I was elated with the cordial and helpful attitude they extended to me.

I was encouraged to pursue the Zeller side of the family; however, I was not without apprehension. One of my first contacts was with the sole surviving Zeller aunt, then eighty-two years old. I scheduled a time to visit her the following Sunday morning in Bayonet Point, Florida, about twenty-four miles north of Clearwater. Together Katie and I visited Aunt Laura Zeller Chase.

Initially, the meeting was cool, somewhat distant, as I recalled the underlying tension within the Zeller family when I was a teenager. Aunt Laura said, "I will help you as much as I can. I got out my records and any papers that I could find."

Aunt Laura and I worked together assembling the family birth dates, dates of death, cemeteries, places and dates of marriages from her notebooks of information, and the atmosphere gradually and steadily warmed up.

Aunt Laura, daughter of Walter Stanley Zeller, would explain, "George, my father moved from Muncie, Indiana, to Rochester, New York, by himself in 1895, when he was sixteen years old. He worked in the factories of the shoe industry in Rochester and married my mother, Florence Clark—your Grandma Zeller—in about 1900."

Around the same time that I spoke with Aunt Laura about the Zeller genealogy, my research in the 1900 Muncie Indiana Census revealed that Grandpa Zeller appeared in the 1900 census and apparently moved to Rochester from Muncie in late 1900 or early 1901, or had moved back to Muncie at some point after 1896. I also learned from the Rochester city directories that my grandfather had lived at seven different residences between 1902 and 1919 prior to purchasing their home on Furlong Street.

....

In 1922, Laura was seven years old and attending Public School #36. Her large family included her parents—Florence, age thirty-eight, and Walter Stanley, forty-three—and two sisters and four brothers. A younger brother, Clayton, had died in the first year of his life from whooping cough.

Their Rochester home had all the conveniences of the times including electricity, running water, indoor plumbing, and central heating. It was located near shopping and a streetcar line. Laura's father worked in the shoe industry and all things were fine. Her brother, Walter Cecil (Cec), my father, was working at Kodak.

In 1923, hard times fell on the shoe industry and the family discussed moving to the country. Florence wanted to buy a small farm in Henrietta on the outskirts of Rochester, but Walter was encouraged by Florence's cousin to buy a farm near Short Tract. Walter went against the wishes of his wife, and in 1924 bought a farm deep in the hills of Short Tract, about sixty miles south of Rochester.

Walter sold their new home on Furlong Street, and also sold his equity in inherited real estate in Perkinsville, Indiana, to his brother Chauncey for a fraction of its value to raise the down payment for the farm. He signed a Contract for Deed for the balance owed on the farm. Walter and Florence were now age forty-five and forty respectively, and Florence was pregnant with her eighth child, Donald, who would be born in July 1924 in Short Tract.

Their oldest daughter, Frances, was now twenty-two years old and working at Peabody's Department Store. She decided not to move to the farm and stayed with friends of the family. The oldest son, Cec, twenty years old, was working at Eastman Kodak but decided to move with the family to the farm.

The Zellers, together with five of their children, Cec, Harold, Clifford, Kenneth, and Laura, drove their 1921 Chevrolet to the farm in Short Tract. However, the house was not livable, as the repairs, including a new floor, had not been completed. So they went to live in Fillmore with a relative. Finally, three months later the work was completed, and they moved to the farm.

The farmhouse had no modern conveniences, no central heat, and no electricity. They used kerosene lamps for light. There was no running water or indoor plumbing; they had a well from which they carried water in buckets to the house, and they used an outhouse.

Cec and Harold found work on farms in the area, and they also worked with crews on threshing machine rigs, going from farm to farm after the wheat, oats, and beans were harvested and brought to the barns. The threshing machine would separate the grain from the pod, and the straw would be blown out the back of the barn to gather in a huge pile. Later, the straw would be carried as needed back into the barn, chicken coop, or pigpen and used for bedding for the cattle, horses, pigs, and chickens.

The ears of corn were stored in a corncrib to dry before the kernels could be shucked from them. Shelled corn and wheat were hauled to the mill in Fillmore to be ground together for a special feed for the chickens and cattle during the winter. Cec and Harold also helped their father on his farm when they could. The family had a lot of chickens and sold eggs as well as chickens. They also sold milk to the cheese factory.

The farming operation did not go well from the beginning, and then it went from bad to worse. Using the 1921 Chevrolet like a truck to haul chicken feed back and forth to Fillmore, about ten miles away, ruined the car. By 1927 everything was chattel mortgaged, and, unfortunately, the Zellers were unable to keep up the payments on equipment and livestock and on the Contract for Deed for the farm.

They lost everything, including the car. There was no sale of the real estate or auction of the equipment and livestock; they just lost everything to the holder of the Contract for Deed for the farm and to the holder of the Chattel Mortgage on the equipment and livestock.

They took a train from Fillmore back to Rochester. Harold, however, decided to stay and work as a hired hand on a local farm, and he never did return to live in Rochester. Eventually, Harold met Leah Rork, a schoolteacher from the Fillmore area. They married in about 1933 and had two children, Gary and Dorance.

From what has been said of the Zeller brothers, Harold and Cec, it seems they were very competitive with each other from early childhood and were constantly at odds with each other, to a point of fault. Both were extremely argumentative and would allow situations to get out of control, after which they would not speak to each other for months at a time. On one occasion several years passed without their speaking to each other.

Now back in Rochester, the Zellers rented half of a double house on Aurora Street, in the old neighborhood, and Grandpa Zeller again found work in the shoe industry.

············

In 1928, Cec, now twenty-five, while working at Robeson Manufacturing Company, met his future wife, Otillia Schmitt, the daughter of the late grocer and successful businessman George J. Schmitt.

On his wedding day, Florence Zeller told her son Cec that if he ever converted to the Catholic religion, she would disown him for life. This difference in religious beliefs caused an unspoken rift between Otillia and her mother-in-law.

The wedding took place in the St. Francis Xavier Roman Catholic Church's Rectory.

My parents rented a small house from Sophia Schmitt, Otillia's mother. Their home, at the corner of Fernwood

Avenue and Portage Street, was one block from the Schmitt family grocery store and two blocks from the Zeller family residence.

When the Zellers went to see their new grandson, Walter, in 1930, my mother—a proud mother and a devout Catholic—in her excitement, announced with joy that she hoped that her first son would be a priest. This did not set well with her mother-in-law and inflamed the sore spot that had existed since the day Otillia married Cec.

This difference in religious beliefs proved to be a major opposition in their relationship throughout the ensuing years and a hurdle they would never be able to get over. Florence's relationship with my mother was always maintained at a distance, and a certain tension always filled the air.

In 1930, Laura, my aunt who later would give me all this valuable information, entered Benjamin Franklin High School on Norton Street, the first year that the school was open. The family was now living on Norton Street.

The country was mired in the Depression now, and her father was laid off; things were very hard. By the end of Laura's freshman year, they had moved to Ridge Road at the corner of Portland Avenue for cheaper rent, and this place was as tough as it was going to get.

Finally, her father found work tending the boilers at night in greenhouses on Titus Avenue perhaps two miles away from home. He was the only one in the family working. Besides his wife Florence, there was now his mother-in-law, Alice Clark Keller, along with his four children still at home, to feed from one paycheck of about $7 per week.

He would walk from Ridge Road and Portland Avenue on the outskirts of Rochester to Tony Zonner's Butcher Shop on Front Street downtown, about six miles, to buy a whole loin of pork for nine cents a pound, and carry it home afoot, for he could not afford the five-cent fare for the streetcar that would have taken him as far as Portland Avenue and Norton Street, about one mile from home.

Aunt Laura recalls that they seemed to move about every year. Genealogy records revealed that eighteen different residences were listed in the Rochester city directories from 1900 to 1955 for Walter S. Zeller.

When Laura was seventeen she met Milo Chase. After their third or fourth date, her mother told her not to see Milo any more as she did not like him. Laura had previous negative experiences with her mother's feelings with other fellows she had dated; after a few dates her mother would find something she didn't like about them and tell Laura that she shouldn't date them any more or tell her she could not go steady with them. Laura really liked Milo and continued to see him, regardless of her mother's objections.

Finally, Laura found a job; she would be working for a lady and her husband in the Cobb's Hill area cleaning house, cooking, taking care of their two small children and doing the washing. For her work, she was paid $4 per week plus room and board. She had Sundays off.

Milo was working as a farm hand for a relative in Spencerport. This made it difficult for the couple to see each other, since Milo did not own an automobile. One day Laura was at the farm of the relative where Milo was working. The lady of the house said she was going to hire someone to do the cleaning and the cooking for the family and the hired hands, as she was going to go to work for a doctor. Laura was tired of her job on Cobb's Hill and saw that a change of jobs would bring her closer to Milo. She talked it over with him and they decided to get married.

They eloped in May 1934. Unfortunately, that weekend it was Milo's weekend to take care of the chores and milk the ·cows, so there was no honeymoon. While Milo did his work, Laura waited. His brother, Milton, showed up and invited Laura to visit her brother Clifford, who was working at Milo's father's farm; Laura said fine, since it was close by. While she was visiting Clifford, her parents arrived with her brother Cec. Laura knew there would be fireworks when her parents learned of her marriage. However, she decided to bite the bullet and get it over with, so she told her parents that she had married Milo Chase.

As Laura had anticipated, the sky burst into fireworks, and her father and mother had some unkind comments for Milo. They told her she would never have anything and that Milo was not welcome in their home. Cec also expressed his two cents worth about Milo, which caused more hard feelings.

In 1938, times were still hard, and Laura and Milo were still living on the farm in Spencerport. In 1940, Milo's brother, Milton, went to school and learned to be a welder and found work at the Pfaudler Company. Milo expressed interest and Milton told him they teach each employee a skill and encouraged Milo to put in an application at Rymington Gould, which was hiring.

A few days later Laura's brother Cec stopped by and Milo told him that he had put an application in. Cec replied, "Milo, what do you know about working in a factory? All you have ever done is walk behind a plow, pulled by a horse; they will never hire you."

But Milo got the job and learned a metal molding process; and later worked on armor plate seven days a week in the war years. The skill he learned was so needed, it kept him out of the draft in World War II.

Later Milo and Laura bought an eighteen-year-old house on Darien Street for $3,800. They borrowed $500 from a bank for the down payment and obtained two mortgages for the balance. The second mortgage holder was satisfied with interest payments only until the first mortgage was paid in full. In the following three years, Milo and Laura saved every dime they could to pay off the mortgages. When they went to make the final payment, they had miscalculated the interest on the balance by $20. So they turned to Laura's parents to borrow the $20 for one week. They were met with a cool reception and then, with great reluctance, Laura's father finally lent them the $20. They promised that when Milo got paid the following Friday they would immediately repay the $20, which they did.

In the ensuing years, Walter Stanley Zeller returned to the shoe industry and worked in various shoe-manufacturing companies in Rochester. However, he was never able to recover financially from losing everything in 1927. He never again was able to purchase a home. He died in 1955 at seventy-six years of age.

....

During our many visits, I learned a great deal more from Aunt Laura about the Zeller family than birth and death dates; my eyes were being opened! She well remembered and expressed the pain and anguish of that period of her life, and it seemed ever present as she told her story. It was the first time that I had heard the story, as I had been led to believe that my father had lived three years on a farm without any adversity and later moved back to Rochester as a young man.

I was finally able to begin to understand the driving force behind my father's obsession with owning the farm in Mumford. I could now begin to explore the effect of the tension that existed between my father and his parents and my father's four younger brothers. This obsession had affected my brother and sister and me so greatly during our growing up!

I remember one of the most severe confrontations between my father and his brother Harold. I was about nine or ten years old when, in 1947, Pa got into a horrendous argument with Harold, and they were at war for several years; they would not talk to each other or even remain in the same place at the same time. Consequently, contact was lost for all of the spouses and cousins during this time.

The two brothers did not speak to each other from about 1947 until 1954. The disagreement was so intense that when either of them was at a family gathering and the other showed up, both families would leave. Little did they know what unthinkable turns in the road lay ahead for each of them. In about 1953 Harold Zeller's wife, Leah, then in her early fifties, contracted breast cancer and suffered with it for several years before dying in 1961.

....

After meeting and getting to know Aunt Laura, I was exhilarated by my experience and persevered in calling all of my cousins on the telephone. I spoke with them and with several of their spouses. It was a joyful experience for me. I was received cordially and was given wonderful cooperation. No one was cool or kept me at a distance, and I never felt the air of tension that I experienced as a child and teenager. I had a wonderful time with Aunt Laura in subsequent visits, now fully convinced that I was not alone in my feelings.

Apparently the tension within the Zeller family had touched all the aunts, uncles and cousins. There always seemed to be a sense of conflict in the air, but not a clear-cut feud like the Hatfields and McCoys. This uncomfortable feeling had a lasting and profound effect on my life. I never again wanted to experience such tension. I had not pursued a normal family relationship with any of my Zeller aunts, uncles or cousins throughout my own marriage and child raising years. I had not contacted any of my Zeller relatives in more than forty years, nor had any of them contacted me.

I felt sorrowful and cheated. My wife, our children, and I had missed out on what could have been a wonderful family relationship with all of the Zeller cousins and all of their children for all those young adult years, now gone and lost forever. I was painfully aware that all of my Zeller relatives had apparently taken a similar path as I had, largely avoiding involvement with each other. Oh, what a price my father and his family paid for his ego!

I think I know now from what basis I developed the saying, "Anything that you can buy or sell doesn't count in a relationship, because anyone else can do that."

I think I know now why I have had no desire to flaunt our success, nor exhibit it in any manner.

I think I know now why I say, you must place your wife on a pedestal, in your mind, on the day that you are married, and that you may never take her off the pedestal, because your commitment will affect the balance of your life.

I think I know now why I say a husband must verbally compliment his wife three times a day. It takes no effort to criticize; it takes real positive thoughts prior to compliment your spouse three times a day, every day. "I love you;" counts as one compliment.

I think I know now why I said to my children in the. course of a serious discussion or disagreement, "I have told you the truth; is there anything that I have told you that I can profit from in any way? Is what I am asking you to do not in your best interest?"

I think I know now why my children said, "You are too protective, Dad."

I think I know now why I have a hard time accepting a sincere compliment.

I have so very much to be thankful for.

As with all of us, not far from the tree does the nut fall. Our experiences alter the course of our lives. We choose the path of our lives and choose to see the glass as half empty or half full. I choose to see the glass half full.

CHAPTER XVIII
My World Darkens,
Then Shines Brightly

In March 1996, after a successful thirty-five-year banking career, of which seventeen-plus years were in Florida, I retired as a vice president from SunTrust Bank at the age of fifty-seven, and Katie retired shortly thereafter from Bank of America in September.

We lived the life of Riley for the next three years, sailing, taking long walks on the beach, traveling, and eventually selling our home in July 1999, so we could do more extensive traveling. We moved into a condo that we owned about a mile from our house in St. Petersburg. In the late fall of 1999, we were walking in Central Park in New York City when my knee went out again. After we returned home I finally decided that after the holidays I would have it taken care of.

Then in January 2000, Katie found a lump in her left breast and went to the doctor to have it checked out. The mammogram showed a spot in the right breast, and a biopsy was scheduled in three weeks. It turned out my left knee surgery was on the day prior to Katie's biopsy, so our son, John, took his mother to the hospital's surgical center.

About five days later the telephone rang about ten a.m. Katie answered the phone, it was her doctor's office, and the nurse said, "The doctor wants to speak with you in his office." Katie scheduled an appointment for that afternoon, hung up the phone and began to cry.

"George, I have breast cancer, that's what the doctor is going to tell me."

I hugged her and said, "Everything is going to be all right--the good Lord is going to take care of you." We both cried as we hugged, as fear of the unknown had taken its grip upon both of us.

I died a thousand deaths; the thought of losing my Katie would destroy my world. Our bright, shining world went dark in an instant, and there seemed to be black clouds everywhere I looked. Was this really happening to my Katie?

The doctor at the appointment just came out with it. "Katie, you have breast cancer; we will have to do surgery and remove the area around the tumor spot and then you will need to have chemotherapy and radiation therapy."

Katie said, "I won't have chemo; I've heard too many bad things about it—I am not going to have chemo."

Waiting was agony; surgery was scheduled to occur in approximately three weeks on Katie's right breast to remove the area around the cancerous spot. Shortly thereafter, despite the insistence of Katie saying, "I will not have chemo," I became more intent on her doing everything possible to help herself. She finally reluctantly agreed; the chemotherapy treatments began as scheduled, and continued for seven treatments, one every three weeks until late July.

Katie was sick throughout the chemotherapy and basically lived on oatmeal and crackers and was so sick that she could not get out of bed most of the time. She slept a great deal each day. The day before the next chemo treatment she would begin to feel somewhat better, and then as soon as she sat down in the chemotherapy treatment room she would get sick again from the smell of the drugs.

As time passed Katie began to lose her hair and over time she would lose all of her beautiful long hair; this had a very negative effect on her and she would cry when she looked into the mirror. I repeatedly said, "Katie, I love you, for you and all about you. Don't worry about your hair; it will grow back in time. I love you, Katie, with all my heart."

She seemed to get sicker with each treatment, and it reached the point that she would not go back to the receiving area even to register for treatment and remained in the waiting area in an adjoining section of the cancer center until they were ready to administer the chemo drug to her.

Katie was so sick after the next-to-the-last scheduled chemo treatment, she cried, and over and over she begged me, "Please, please let me quit this chemo program; I am so sick, don't make me take another treatment."

I felt terrible for her, and understood her feelings and felt her pain and anguish daily as I witnessed for months how sick she was. I sympathized with Katie; however, I could not in good conscience let her quit the chemo program with just one treatment to go.

"Katie, you are dealing with your life and also with my happiness," I said. "The good Lord will help you through the last of the effects of these treatments and you will be done with it forever; and you will know that you have done all that you can do to help yourself. I love you so much, Katie."

On the morning of the seventh and final treatment, she looked at me, smiled softly with tears in her eyes and said, "Let's go." She was terribly sick, but she completed the chemotherapy program.

Throughout these long months, I kept myself busy with our family genealogy. In the second bedroom of the condo I had set up my office, and made numerous telephone calls, wrote hundreds of letters and did research on the Internet using ancestry.com and rootsweb.com. I entered all of the family information found into the genealogy program, Family Tree Maker. By the time the chemo treatments were completed our family tree had grown to upwards of 4,500 names on file.

....

Following chemotherapy, radiation treatments were scheduled to begin two weeks later: thirty-four consecutive treatments. Radiation was much different, Katie was never sick; we went daily to the Cancer Center at St. Anthony's Hospital at nine a.m, and from the time we arrived until the time we left, rarely were we there longer than a total of twenty minutes.

Katie began to eat regular food again, except for citrus and in particular lemon-flavored anything. We purchased several wigs and she gradually became more comfortable wearing them in public. I had become so accustomed to seeing her as bald as a cue ball, she was as beautiful to me as she always had been. I did not see her as a bald person; what I saw was Katie, my Katie.

One day she was feeling pretty good so she went with me to the grocery store, we walked up and down the aisles talking while we shopped for the better part of an hour. Both of us were completely unaware that she had forgotten to put on her wig before we left home, completely unaware of it the entire time we did our shopping. As we were just about through the checkout line I was paying the clerk, when I realized it; a few minutes later apparently Katie realized it as she placed her hand up by her ear.

Her eyes filled with tears and she was immediately full of stress; I put my arm around her; and said, "Katie, I'm sorry I forgot to remind you to wear your wig when we left, but I am so used to seeing you without it that I did not notice. I love you for you, just as you are... you are beautiful to me just as you are... please don't worry about it."

She wiped her tears away and we went home.

. . . .

In late September, we decided to take a vacation a few days after the last radiation treatment. We drove up to New England to see the leaves change color. Katie did fine on the three-week trip, the weather cooperated with clear sunny days, and we enjoyed the change of pace while seeing many breathtaking views highlighted by the beautiful fall colors as we drove through the Catskill Mountains into the wine country of the Finger Lakes region and then up through the Adirondacks Mountains.

One morning in Plattsburg, we took the car ferry across Lake Champlain into Vermont and then drove to a resort in Franconia Notch, New Hampshire, in the White Mountains. Later we drove around Mount Washington and through the Berkshire Mountains in Massachusetts and through the mountains and the deep valleys of New England and up the back roads to Bar Harbor, Maine. We admired the magnificent colors of the leaves, the ever-changing landscapes of the countryside with creeks and babbling brooks, and witnessing these scenes, we realized that they are truly the kingdoms of Heaven on Earth to be admired by all.

On our last day in New Hampshire, it was twenty-eight degrees, fine snow was in the air and the wind swirled the snow around on this brisk morning when I put our luggage in the car. It was our signal that it was time to point the car south toward the palm trees of Florida and warm waters of the Gulf of Mexico and to our home. Shortly after returning home, the effects of the radiation kicked in and Katie would become extremely tired in an instant and needed to lie down and sleep; she slept a great deal during the next year.

In January 2002 during my annual physical, the doctor discovered some irregularities in my electrocardiogram and in the PSA blood test. He suspected a heart attack and sent me immediately to the emergency room. After a series of tests I was referred to a cardiologist, and in early February she performed a cardiac cath and found eighty-five percent blockage in one artery, which required a stent to be implanted a couple of days later.

Four days after I returned home from the hospital, the phone rang, Katie answered and the call was for me. "George, it's the nurse from the urologist's office and she wants to speak to you," said Katie.

I took the phone from her and said, "This is George," and the nurse told me, "The doctor wants to see you in the office this afternoon." I scheduled a time to meet with the doctor.

Katie heard the conversation and started to cry; she put her arms around me and said, "Oh no, not you too, George, Oh, God, what is happening to us?"

I told Katie, "Don't worry, everything will be okay; the good Lord will take care of me, just like he took care of you."

The PSA blood test showed a substantial increase in one year, from two-point-two to three-point-zero, or about a thirty-six percent increase, though well below the normal concern level of four-point-zero. With the significant upward percentage increase in the PSA, I had insisted on a prostate biopsy that showed cancer in one of the twelve samples. After meeting with two oncologists I decided on a seed implant. Because I was taking a blood-thinning drug, Plavix, for my heart condition, that I needed to be free of before the procedure, we had to wait until April 1 for the seed implant.

I experienced no sickness like Katie did; nothing at all like Katie—four days after the seed implant she and I went sailing on Tampa Bay and had a great time. Perhaps a month later I experienced something similar to hot flashes and became overwhelmingly tired in an instant, and this required that I lie down immediately for maybe an hour or so. As time passed this situation gradually passed during the year.

Everything seemed to be going along fine until late November when I required right knee surgery. Then, in December, I became very short of breath. Back to the cardiologist I went, and we scheduled another cardiac cath, resulting in an angioplasty, which was needed to clean out the stent. Since then we have had several significant issues occur, but all were resolved without any major incidents.

It is now approaching November 1, 2008, and Katie and I are doing fine, both cancer survivors and enjoying our retirement immensely.

CHAPTER XIX

Dear Walter, Continued

I wanted to help my brother to find his way to free himself of his agony and tormented memories of our father's grip on his life. I was over fifty years old before I was free of the troubled memories of my father and his fierce domination of my life; and it only happened by chance.

Over and over Walter had said to me, "George, no matter how hard I have tried, I can not shake myself free of my plaguing memories of Pa's harshness towards me during my youth on the farm."

I had repeatedly failed in my prior attempts to share with my brother the information I had learned about the truth of Ma's medical condition and information about Pa that I had learned in my genealogy research. In all of my previous encounters and efforts to try and talk with Walter, he would not listen, took over the conversation and negated my efforts.

I decided I would try again and perhaps the best way that I might be able to help him was to write him a letter providing him with the genealogy information that I had learned over the past fifteen years and the medical information about the severe effects of menopause that I had learned from doctors. I would also explain to him in detail about my life on the farm for the eight years after Walter had moved on; so he would understand he was not alone with these troubling memories.

I thought perhaps if he could sit down and read my letter, think about the information provided, re-read it and think about it more, then maybe he would talk about it, if he wanted to. I hoped the information might help him to find some understanding that he was not aware of; and hopefully he could find forgiveness in his heart and peace in his life and be free at last.

Unfortunately, he became extremely angry after receiving my letter. He considered it an invasion into his life, not an effort to help him. On February 28, 2006, Katie and I drove up to Rochester to attend the funeral of her brother in law Charlie Morreale. While in Rochester I called Walter and drove across town to meet him at a restaurant for coffee near his home. Walter was totally unwilling to discuss any of the information in the letter about him, Pa or about Ma's illness.

He hardly spoke to me at the restaurant and then only about weather-related meaningless subjects. Then he continued his silence, his form of punishment, barely speaking to me for the next eighteen months; a punishment style he had learned from our father. When he did call, he had a routine; he said what he wanted to say; was not interested in hearing any conversation from me, and then quickly ended the conversation and hung up.

JMJ

December 7, 2005

My Dear Brother Walter... (continued)

I hope this letter finds you well, and in good spirits. I am sincerely concerned about you, and I hope I can help you with what I have observed and what I have learned during the past twelve years. Walter, as you have been quite sensitive toward any of my comments or suggestions, I had great concern about writing this letter to you, so, before I wrote the letter to you, I first asked for the divine guidance of our Lord, Jesus Christ.

Throughout your life, Walter, you have accomplished so very much, raising and educating seven children, a stellar record, a cut way above the average, so much to be proud of. Your life has been a complete dedication to your children and your work. In your retirement, your community spirit was evident in the gift of your time and energy for years of selfless work to aid strangers by serving as a volunteer at the Red Cross. In addition, your service to the Catholic grammar schools as a fourth-grade math mentor in several different schools, several sessions each week, had a very positive effect on the future of many children. Also for many years you have given your time and have served at funeral masses, not an easy thing to do.

Yes, Walter, you are a very special person indeed. Very few people are willing, and even fewer are capable of performing the volunteer service that you have. Few can give of themselves unselfishly as you have done.

In addition, in your willingness to step up to the plate and aid our father's second wife, Lillian, you did everything possible for her in her declining years, watching over her and her finances at the assisted living facility, Dunn Towers, after which you found a good complete care nursing home for Lillian and took care of all the arrangements for her and even cleaned out her old apartment at Dunn Towers. You watched over her in the hospital, and took care of all the arrangements and finances for her admission, including all the paperwork required by government agencies. And then you worked out all the final arrangements for Lillian. You did all of this with no one asking you; you saw the need that existed and filled it, giving freely of yourself.

You have been doing all these things and going at breakneck speed for a very long time now. In addition, you've been dealing with all the demands of taking care of your own wife, Rose, who also has significant health problems. Yes, Walter, you are a very special person, indeed.

However, one thing that I have observed that has put a blemish on all of your joy, daily happiness, and accomplishments is your nagging memories of our father that you cannot seem to shake. I also suffered deeply for many years with my agonizing memories of Pa before I was able to forgive him and be totally free of his grip on my life. The purpose of my writing this letter is not to critique you, but to try to help you free yourself of this agony so that you can more fully enjoy the balance of your life, the beautiful part that through your uniqueness you have created.

I do not believe that Pa acted toward us as he did on a premeditated basis. However, Pa responded to the pressure of his life. Yes, it was pressure he created for himself, a result of his poor and selfish decision to buy the farm without a thorough investigation and without consideration of how this decision would affect his wife or family. Pa's actions towards us on the farm demonstrated his frustrations, not a conscious decision to abuse us. Pa acted totally without consideration toward us. He did not consider his responsibility to us. He was unaware of his negative thoughts, words, and actions. It would appear he was totally unaware of the pain and hurt that he inflicted on his wife, our mother, and each of his children.

I sincerely believe the following information that I found on the Internet about forgiveness is true, and I hope you will also find it helpful.

"If we really want to love, we must learn how to forgive." - Mother Theresa

Forgiveness works! It is often difficult!

Non-forgiveness keeps you in the struggle. Being willing to forgive can bring a sense of peace and well-being. It lifts anxiety and delivers you from depression. It can enhance your self-esteem and give you hope.

Forgive and forget is a myth. You may never forget AND you can choose to forgive. As life goes on and you remember, then is the time to once again remember that you have already forgiven. Mentally forgive again if necessary, and then move forward. When we allow it, time may dull the vividness of the memory of the hurt; the memory might fade.

Forgiveness is a creative act that changes us from prisoners of the past to liberated people at peace with our memories. It is not forgetfulness, but it involves accepting the promise that the future can be more than dwelling on memories of past injury. Choice is always present in forgiveness. You do not have to forgive AND there are consequences. Refusing to forgive by holding on to the anger, resentment and a sense of betrayal can make your own life miserable. A vindictive mind-set creates bitterness and lets the betrayer claim one more victim.

When you forgive you do it for you, not for the other. The person you have never forgiven. . .owns you!

Walter, please listen to me. Even though I am eight years younger than you, I am sixty-seven years old and retired—not quite a kid any more. I would honestly like to try to help you, though I know that you do not want my help. I know there was a significant age difference when we were kids. I also understand this may be difficult for you to listen to and, God forbid, take advice from your younger brother.

Please be patient with me; I will try to share with you my feelings on the subject of forgiving Pa. I know I tried earnestly to share them with you when I flew up in the summer of 1996, and several times since, but you were not able at the time to listen with an open mind.

Walter, you said what you wanted to say, as it related to you, and that was the extent of your interest in a discussion. In other words, Walt, you would not listen with an open mind, and repeatedly interrupted me, choosing to reiterate all the mistakes you thought Pa had made. You detailed the harsh, nasty, unfair treatment you received on the farm from Pa between November 1945 and June 1948, and expressed your enduring agony that festers like a wound that refuses to heal.

In September 2005, I was once again in the Rochester area, this time for my fiftieth class reunion. While in Rochester we shared dinner together on a few occasions. At the end of our time in Rochester, you and your wife Rose graciously took Katie and me to the Red Osier Restaurant in nearby Stafford for a lovely meal. After dinner, you asked us to meet you at the old farm in Mumford, about thirteen miles away. I had little interest in revisiting the farm, as I knew it was in a declining state of repair. However I agreed, and was aware that it would be close to dark by the time we drove there.

It is now over fifty years since I have lived on the farm in Mumford, and I have been there on several occasions with you. We arrived at the farm shortly before dark. Once again, Walter, you acknowledged that you come back to the old farm on a regular basis, and then began your litany of the things you felt Pa did wrong, making your point that Pa could have done better for you. I told you it was time for you to set it aside and make your peace with our father, as he has been dead now for almost twenty-one years.

To try and make my point, Walter, I told you I realize that I am not perfect either and have made my share of mistakes. If you were to ask my kids what they think of their dad as a father and about their lives growing up, I am sure, if they were honest with you, they would offer several negative comments and judgments on how I should have done some things differently, or how I should not have said some things that I did. I told you that is normal and occurs in almost all families.

In an attempt to further make my point to you, I told you, Walter, I am sure if I were to ask your kids, what if any criticism they might have of their father, if they were honest, they would have plenty to say. You replied, "Not my kids. My kids think I am perfect in every way. I did everything right!"

Walter, you were not joking; you were dead serious. You bristled, and then folded your arms over your chest and set your feet as though you were preparing to physically defend yourself. I quickly realized that I had hit your hot button, and nothing good would come of any additional comments on the subject. We said our goodnights and you drove off quickly.

It was at that time, that I became totally aware that your visits to the old farm were a feeding frenzy for you. It appears that these visits rejuvenate your anger toward Pa as you review the litany of things that disturb you about our father. I cannot understand for what reason you continue to do this. The physical appearance of the farm today is nothing like it was when I left home at age seventeen in 1955. It is now run down, the outbuildings are falling down, and the fields have returned to the wild, not having felt the touch of a plow for more than fifty years.

Your adamant position about being perfect reminded me of Pa and his ways. He was always so sure he was right, wasn't he? But do you honestly think you were perfect as a father? And are we required to be perfect? Ask your children! Your children are grown up now; they won't be afraid to give you an honest answer. Don't be surprised at what you might hear, and don't be afraid either. We are not expected to be perfect.

I know you were a wonderful father, devoted to your children, and did your very best with your seven children in every way, but no father is perfect—no human being is perfect. As long as you feel that you were and are a perfect father in contrast to the behavior of your own father, I doubt that anyone can help you rid yourself of the agony you recall from 1945 to 1948. I cannot help you find peace with the memory of our father as you continue to demonstrate over and over again that you do not want peace.

For whatever reason, and after over fifty-seven years have passed since you lived on the farm, you obviously receive some significant satisfaction in regularly visiting the farm in Mumford and recalling a litany of mistakes of Pa, the nastiness, harshness that you feel you endured at the hands of our father. I know the harshness was real, because I witnessed it, but that was more than fifty years ago. Understanding this obsession of yours, one may reach this question: Walter, are you comparing yourself and your accomplishments to our father's?

Please let me share with you my overview on this subject of forgiving Pa. I grew up on the same farm with the same father as you did, from the age of seven to seventeen. Then I moved out on my own, to the YMCA in Rochester. I did not have a bed of roses either. I hated Pa with all my heart. I thought he was the nastiest, meanest, cruelest man I had ever met. But I forgave him many years ago, and I tried to use what I didn't like about him to help me in developing my life, as you obviously have done too.

I hated his negative attitude: He could not be happy for others' good fortune, only his own. He often bragged about how good he was while he knocked virtually everyone else. He took credit that was due to others. He was not willing to listen to others or respect their points of view; he seldom showed consideration for others' desires. He was generally cantankerous and stubborn. I hated his methods and his controlling ways. As you well remember, it was his way or no way. In other words, I learned very important lessons from Pa: what not to be like! I have been fighting some of these traits all of my adult life and have failed on many occasion. I had wonderful mentors in my in-laws; by their actions they taught me much about life, trust, and love.

But, Walter, in my genealogy research, I also learned some of the things that drove Pa and contributed to his poor decision-making. I now know about his own father's bad decision to buy a farm in Short Tract against his wife's wishes, and his subsequent failure, resulting in financial ruin for life. That happened when our Pa was twenty years old. In 1927, Grandpa Zeller and his family returned, destitute, to Rochester, never regaining prior financial status. While Pa returned with his parents, his brother, Harold, remained in the Short Tract area working as a hired hand on farms.

Although strangers easily led our Pa, he would rarely listen to suggestions from his wife and immediate family who truly cared. He always knew it all! Often Pa acted alone, and in haste. His unfulfilled need to be recognized and rewarded with praise from his parents and four brothers had a terrible effect on our family, and this was coupled with the never-ending competition from inside his family. These insights help me better understand how Pa got like he was and the limitations on his ability to behave any differently.

Throughout the twelve years of Ma's illness, ending with her suicide in May 1967, I wrongfully and adamantly blamed Pa for Ma's mental illness and for her death. I never stopped telling Pa how I felt. I fervently believed that Pa's harsh treatment of Ma over the years was the cause of her mental illness. I had nothing but contempt for Pa. I was brutal in my judgment and comments to his face and behind his back. I know you can imagine how I felt, Walter.

In 1992, I was stunned to learn that Pa was not at all responsible for Ma's illness. Yes, that's right: Pa did not cause, nor was he responsible in anyway, for Ma's mental health problems. Pa did not drive Ma into a mental condition. Ma suffered from Acute Menopause as millions of other women suffered with it in the 1950s in the USA. I discovered this medical condition when my wife went through menopause. The look in her eyes was the same glassy, forlorn look as I had seen in Ma's eyes in 1955, when I pulled her out of Oatka Creek near the old swimming hole.

In 1992, two doctors explained the seriousness of menopause to me, and separately each doctor told me of the severe effects of it on their own mothers. Both doctors told me how their mothers were locked up in state mental institutions that looked like prisons. One doctor told me that his mother committed suicide, as thousands of women had. Both doctors explained how little was known medically about women's problems and menopause at that time.

Thousands of women were thought to have serious mental problems and were locked up for life across the USA.

Today I understand that menopause is routinely handled with medicine quite successfully. Unfortunately, Walter, I learned too late about the effects of menopause on Ma. Yes, too late, too late for me to apologize to Pa and ask for his forgiveness for my many years of brutal and totally wrong judgment of him. It was too late to apologize for my mean and totally unwarranted comments to him and about him over many years. Yes, too late to ask for his forgiveness! Pa died February 14, 1985, seven years before I learned about menopause being the cause of Ma's illness. This I regret with all my heart!

By searching out my memories and history of our family, I have been able to find some understanding and make some sense of why our family had so little closeness and harmony. First of all, I don't remember seeing or even hearing from Ma, Mary Ann, or you, or the uncles or aunts in the Schmitt family, about any nastiness or harsh treatment by Pa before our family moved to the farm in Mumford. Yes, I did hear plenty about how hard the times were, but not about any mean behavior by Pa.

I understand that, independently of his family, and without thorough investigation, Pa, just as his father had done before him, decided to buy the farm in Mumford in 1945 and fulfill his dream. This decision was made without the blessing of his wife. Unfortunately, his ill-conceived plan could not be easily changed. This decision proved to be irreversible, and we had to live with it and suffer its consequences. Sometimes people do not perform well under pressure or in a bad situation, which they have created. They cannot admit they have made such a major mistake in judgment.

Consequently, this decision resulted in Pa's lashing out at us and indirectly or inadvertently placing the blame and responsibility on his family. Pa was never able to admit his bad decision and talk about his feelings in order to gain the understanding of his family. The price he paid for his actions was the loss of his children's love.

We as children, as teenagers, and later as adults never felt the love of our father, nor did we have any joy in seeing him or hearing from him. For years as an adult I choose to block out most memories of my youth. Busy with my family and career, I thought I had successfully buried the pain, embarrassment, and shame of my youth. The past was so unpleasant that I chose to block out most of my teenage years. Later I learned that gathering information about the past, even though very painful, was the only way to gain understanding with maturity. Finally I was able to forgive Pa for all his nastiness. Walter, at that moment I felt wonderful; a great weight had been lifted off my back! Almost instantly, I began to feel pity for Pa because of all the beautiful and tender experiences of life that he had cheated himself out of.

Remembering is the only way to begin to understand and, together with knowledge of the past, it will eventually allow one to forgive and then to heal.

It may be well to reflect for a moment upon the words of the late Pope John Paul II: "The worst prison would be a closed heart."

Walter, it is time to let go of your hurt, and it is time to forgive our father and find your peace and fully enjoy your remaining years. Please stop going out to the old farm in Mumford! Bear in mind, the true meaning of family should be about love, forgiveness and sacrifice, not competition. Please remember: if you can buy it or sell it, it does not count; any one can do that. Time is short and so very precious, particularly at our stage in life.

···

In her best-selling book, The Measure of Success, *Marian Wright Edelman has a chapter entitled "A Letter to My Sons." It includes the following extraordinary paragraph. Perhaps it could have been from Pa to you, Walter, if he only knew how to say it.*

Son,

"I seek your forgiveness for all the times I talked when I should have listened; got angry when I should have been patient; acted when I should have waited; feared when I should have been delighted; scolded when I should have encouraged; criticized when I should have complimented; said no when I should have said yes and said yes when I should have said no. I did not know a whole lot about parenting or how to ask for help. I often tried too hard and wanted and demanded so much, and mistakenly sometimes tried to mold you into my image of what I wanted you to be rather than discovering and nourishing you as you emerged and grew."

In his book, Soul Mates, *Thomas Moore wrote, "Our task as adults then might be to search for whatever it takes to forgive our parents for being imperfect. In some families, that imperfection will be slight, in others severe, but in any case we have to deal with evil and suffering in our own lives without the benefit of a scapegoat. In fact, our lives would be all richer if we could let go of the excuse of parental failure... Thinking negatively and pathologically about the family distances us from family members and we lose the opportunity to be enriched by them."*

Harold Kushner writes in his book, How Good Do We Have To Be, *"In the beginning, in the infancy of the human race as in the infancy of an individual human being, life was simple. Then we ate the fruit of that tree and we gained knowledge that some things are good and others are bad. We learned how painfully complex life could be. But at the end, if we are brave enough to love, if we are strong enough to forgive, if we are generous enough to rejoice in another's happiness, and if we are wise enough to know that there is enough love to go around for us all, then we can achieve a fulfillment that no other living creature will ever know. We can reenter Paradise."*

In Abounding Grace, *M. Scott Peck, M.D., quotes Cardinal John Henry Newman: "We can believe what we choose. We are answerable for what we choose to believe."*

Matthew 6:12,14,15-12—"Forgive us the wrongs we have done, as we forgive the wrongs that others have done to us..." 14—"If you forgive others the wrongs they have done to you, your Father in heaven will also forgive you." 15—"But if you do not forgive others, then your Father will not forgive the wrongs you have done."

...

Walter, I strongly encourage you to speak with an older doctor about the history of menopause and the limited medical treatments available to Ma in 1955 as well as the current treatment of women experiencing menopause today.

I am sure that if Ma and Pa could see you and your family now, Walter, they would be the proudest of parents and grandparents. You have accomplished more in your life than you ever dreamed possible.

May God bless you abundantly throughout your life! As the priest said in church on Sunday, be sure to keep Jesus in your Christmas. See you in church.

Thank you, Walter, for reading my lengthy letter. I hope you find some information that you can use to your benefit.

I love you, Walter, so please listen.

> *Your Brother,*
>
> *George*

CHAPTER XX

It's Time To Tack

Now in 2008, I have finally realized and accepted the fact that I cannot help my brother to heal his wounds. I have decided it is best that, whenever Walter brings up the farm in Mumford and talks about how the barns are further deteriorating, I do not comment but rather try to change the topic. It is obvious that Walter finds comfort somehow in revisiting the farm and the painful memories of his youth while thinking about how his father could have done things differently and helped him more.

I am truly sorry that I was unable to help Walter find the same peace I had finally been able to feel. I still have hope though; and I ask and trust God to help Walter find peace in his life and love in his heart.

I have grown to realize that my life, like yours, is a story in motion that has seen many seasons of change; accompanied by hidden bends and twists like those in a creek, enabling the complexity of the journey of life to unfold gradually in finding serenity in its time, as the water. in the creek finds its way to the sea.

(Photo by Dawn Seger)

The old farm buildings as they are today—October 2008

. . . .

There is an old story about an Indian grandfather talking privately with his grandson by the side of a lake. His grandson tells him of his anger concerning several students in his class who have done mean things to him and called him nasty names for no reason at all. The grandfather listens intently as his grandson speaks, replying that he too had been angered many times while he was growing up. He speaks of all the work he had done and how hard he had tried to please, of how all his efforts had gone unnoticed, only more work being given to him. He expresses his frustration at the way he had been treated.

The grandfather explains how he struggled with all of these feelings of hate for a very long time, even though he has realized that his hatred affects only him, and not the one that has caused his pain.

Grandfather then speaks about the two mountain lions inside of him. One lion is nice. He is happy with life. He minds his own business, gets along fine, is truthful, honest and kind to others, does not look for trouble, and fights only if attacked. The other mountain lion is always looking for trouble, always angry with everyone. The slightest thing sets him off in a rage. He is selfish and cruel to everyone and fights with everyone. His rage is so great he cannot think.

The grandfather then tells his grandson: "It is very hard to live with both of these mountain lions inside of me, as both lions want to rule me."

The young boy looks up at his grandfather and asks, "Which one wins, Grandfather?"

The grandfather puts his hand on his grandson's shoulder and gently says, "The one I feed."

CHAPTER XXI

Our Life,
Beyond My Father's Farm

To this point my memoirs have largely focused on stories of my growing up years, the challenges, troubles, illness, and tragedy of my mother; the decisions, the cantankerous mannerisms, nastiness, and insensitive attitude of my father that had prolonged negative effects on each child in the Zeller family.

I looked back at my search for love and eventually finding it; the early years of our marriage; the amazing discoveries thirty years later, finding answers about the mystery of my mother's illness and the basis of my father's dream; examining my negative feelings towards my father; and eventually finding forgiveness. And also, my numerous failed efforts to try to help my brother free himself of his tormented memories of our father's grip on his life; and finally my realization that I could not help my brother, as only he can help himself.

. . . .

I too am far from perfect and have made more than my share of mistakes and I ask the good Lord each day to help me to not make so many. In writing this book I have visited those painful memories in great detail and the tears have rolled down my face, oh so many days, but I honestly think that this experience also had real therapeutic value to me.

I still vividly remember his effect on my life, but I no longer hate my father; actually I have nothing but pity for him; as he cheated himself out of all the beauty of the love of his wife, the innocence of his children throughout their growing-up years, the pleasure of his children as adults, and the joy of his grandchildren; as he totally missed out on the beauty and purpose of life itself.

....

Enjoying the pleasures of retirement with not a care in the world, and then experiencing the sudden jolt of being told of Katie's cancer, brought into clear focus for me the fear and awareness of how fragile life is. Surviving our bouts with serious health problems, we realized how precious our love and our relationship are; and our total awareness of the depth of our love and our faith. The joy we felt, when each other's health was restored, led us to our commitment to celebrate our lives together each and every day.

With the poignant awareness that one day this beautiful relationship will end, we are fully aware of the emptiness the survivor will experience, a living Hell on Earth. I sincerely, selfishly hope that I will pass first as I cannot bear to think of my life without my Katie as she has made my life complete; as she has been the center of my world forever.

When I look back at our lives together prior to and during our retirement years, I can definitely state: Of all my business decisions, taking an early retirement was my best!

When I first retired, my neighbor Harley, age ninety-one, stopped over to congratulate me and told me about what I might expect in retirement; he had traveled all over the world with his wife, Dorothy of sixty five years, during his retirement. Harley said, "George, first you will Go Go, then you will Go Slow, and finally you will No Go, so enjoy yourself as long as you can gooooooooooooooooooo."

Our day-to-day simple lifestyle did not change much as life just goes on; love was the motto of our home. We could always count on each other; there was never a doubt if the other person would be there for whatever reason. We were still lovers and best friends and talked about everything. We continued to do just about everything together, as we always did throughout our marriage, and at Katie's business, while each of us also had separate interests and involvement away from home.

We understood the value and need of a positive attitude in doing a lot of things together and approached the reality, and sometimes the necessity that either of us be able to help the other and pick up the slack if need be at any time for any reason--like make dinner... do the laundry... do the shopping... do the dishes... try to understand the finances... pay the bills... change a diaper... clean the bathroom... read a story to the kids... bake a cake... sail the boat... chart a course... help the kids with their homework... cut the grass... vacuum the rug... listen to the kids read a story to you... check the oil in the car... listen to your children's problems... polish the stainless on the boat... play basketball with the kids or listen to them practice the organ.

In other words, be largely interchangeable in the operation of a happy home, and try—even if not always successfully—to be gentle and friendly to your spouse with a smile on your face even when the pressure of job, home, and finances has you stretched to the limit.

During our working careers as a family we always enjoyed togetherness, at family outings we often ate in lots of neighborhood restaurants and shared many ice creams as we walked and talked. Our vacations were limited by time and the seasonal constraints of Katie's business; they were generally water related; on the sailboat, a cabin in a state park, and winter vacations on the beaches in Florida.

....

Throughout twelve-plus years of our retirement Katie and I truly have had a ball, with the exception of a couple of years of medical interruptions. Now with the availability of time, we have begun to take more vacations away from sailing the waters of the Gulf of Mexico and expanded our horizons. Traveling by car we have criss-crossed the United States several times, visiting many of the places of interest like the Grand Canyon, the Painted Desert, Las Vegas, Yosemite, Yellowstone, Bryce, and Zion National Parks, to name a few.

We have driven up and down both coasts along the back roads from Key West, Florida, to Halifax, Canada, enjoying the quaintness of Savannah, Georgia, and the southern charm of Beaufort and Charleston, S.C.; riding the car ferries on the Chesapeake; enjoyed the beauty of the fall in New England, walking in Central Park and eating in Chinatown in New York City; stopping at the Liberty Bell and eating a Philly cheese steak sandwich and enjoying a beer in Philadelphia; visiting the battlefield at Gettysburg, the Naval Academy at Annapolis, Maryland, and our nation's capitol in Washington, D.C.

Over years on various trips driving along the west coast from San Diego, California, to Monterey, Carmel and the Big Sur region, to San Francisco, to the awesome rugged coast of Oregon, to Pike's Place Fish Market and enjoying the ferry rides across Puget Sound in Seattle. We enjoyed the delicious seafood chowder and halibut fish dinners in the quaint city of Bellingham, Washington; the incredible drive on Highway 99 from the Washington state/Canadian border along Puget Sound with sailing yachts on our left and the towering snow-covered Canadian Rockies on our right, known as the Swiss Alps of America. The view from the cable car ride to the top of the ski slopes in the Canadian Rockies at Whistler, B.C., was beyond our imagination.

In our travels we have enjoyed many of the back roads of Alabama and its cotton fields and the rice fields of Louisiana, the beignets and coffee at Café Du Monde in New Orleans, and have driven the back roads and enjoyed the town parks along the banks of the Mississippi River from New Orleans to its head waters north of Minneapolis, Minnesota. We drove up and over the top of Lake Superior through Canada to Sault Ste. Marie, Michigan, and on to the Golden Dome and the Basilica of the Sacred Heart at Notre Dame in West Bend, Indiana, where we were allowed to attend the ordination of a Catholic priest, a very moving and uplifting experience in our lives.

We have enjoyed driving many miles of the quiet roads and rolling hills of Amish country in Ohio and Pennsylvania; and we've eaten many lunches from our cooler along the waterways and in town parks, and sometimes off the trunk lid of the car along the way. On all of these trips we had a general direction in mind, we just pointed the car in that direction and left, with no schedule, no reservations, no time table, no anticipation of what we were going to see or experience.

Sometimes we were gone for only one, two or three weeks, on other trips we were gone up to three and a half months; we stopped when we were tired, stayed when we found something interesting to enjoy, and paid our bills using the Internet facilities in the nearest town library. We have found it is more fun to travel and just enjoy each day and let each day develop; rather than maintain a schedule.

Throughout my forty-one-year employment career I maintained a rigorous schedule with accountability; this is not for me in retirement as I have nothing to accomplish but enjoy all this free time of each day to its fullest. During a week visit to San Francisco we spent a whole Saturday just walking across the Golden Gate Bridge watching for hours several sailboat races from above; and experienced first hand the vast fluctuations in the temperature and wind speed of San Francisco Bay; then we walked back across the bridge to the city by the bay. Later we visited nearby Muir Woods National Park and spent an afternoon walking amongst the incredible and magnificent giant redwood trees.

The only state we have not visited is North Dakota and hopefully one day we will drive there. We have cruised to most of the islands in the Caribbean, and from Valparaiso, Chile, the port city for Santiago up along the west coast of South America, visiting several ports in Chile and Peru and through the Panama Canal. On one motor trip out West, Katie called the travel agent and arranged a last-minute back-to-back cruise for the inside passage to Alaska. We have taken numerous Mediterranean and transatlantic cruises as well as toured many European countries by train on our own and by bus with tour companies in Europe.

Last fall our longest overseas endeavor encompassed seven-plus weeks, including a three-week train trip on our own in Europe. We visited Florence, Italy, Zermatt, Switzerland, and took three cable cars to the highest point up the Matterhorn, and rode the Glacier Express and the Bernia Express through the Swiss Alps; visited the castle that Disney copied near Fuessen, Germany, before meeting German relatives in Munich and having a beer at the

Haufbrauhouse, relatives we had met by chance in 2001 in Iffezheim while tracing the steps of our ancestors; then joining a tour group in Munich for a ten-day tour to Prague, Budapest, Vienna and Salzburg.

We took the train from Munich to Montecatini, Italy, a nine-hour ride with no changes; the route provided an awesome view of the Swiss and Italian Alps. We visited Pisa, Lucca, Siena and San Gimignano prior to going to Rome before beginning a transatlantic cruise; the last port we visited prior to crossing the Atlantic was Funchal, Portugal, in the Madeira Islands, and we experienced the thrill of riding the toboggan (straw basket) down from Monte—what a ride, never to be forgotten.

I have to admit that for the three-week-plus portion of the trip while we were on our own, beginning in Florence, Italy, we had prepared a detailed schedule of where to be and often followed a somewhat rigid timetable to be sure we did not miss trains and pre-arranged tours; as them trains don't wait for no one!

Back home in our own back yard during our retirement we continued to enjoy sailing early on until our health dictated a change in menu; no regrets as we had the pleasure of sailing for a total of thirty-five years; the first ten years sailing mostly on our Islander 23 in the evening hours on Lake Ontario except for sailing vacations to U.S. ports and to all the Canadian ports on the lake; and then for twenty-five years on our Columbia 8.7 sailboat in the warm waters of Tampa Bay and the Gulf of Mexico, as far south as the Dry Tortugas and Key West.

Sailing on—George and Katie on their sailboat

We still enjoy the easygoing outdoor lifestyle and the warm and generally accommodating weather of Florida. We have walked every foot along the thirty-five miles of white sand beaches on the Gulf of Mexico from the Pass-A-Grille Pass, which is adjacent to Egmont Key at the mouth of Tampa Bay, to Blind Pass on the north end of Clearwater Beach; and also on most of the beaches south of St. Petersburg to Marco Island. We've vacationed at numerous resorts on the beaches from Clearwater to Marco Island and Key West, enjoying the lovely sunrises and glorious sunsets.

I have found the Internet to be a wonderful source to learn from and to help me in seeking out new places to see and make travel plans as we continue to enjoy our simple quiet lifestyle to the fullest.

The good Lord has blessed us abundantly throughout our lives with so much love, happiness, and good health in ·our marriage and with everything we ever needed and more than we could have ever imagined; he has provided us with the most fantastic views of nature and with thousands of Kingdoms of Heaven here on earth to enjoy and marvel about; some beyond words to describe.

We have so much to be thankful for; I have lived with so much love in my marriage that is beyond my fondest dreams. To love Katie is wonderful, but to have experienced her love and being loved by Katie is marvelous and has made my life complete. Jesus answered our prayers with a burning love, enabling us to love each other a thousand times more than we did on the day when I gave Katie her engagement ring in St. Jerome's Catholic Church so many years ago.

Recently we celebrated our forty-seventh wedding anniversary; we are still in love, but with a much deeper love and appreciation of our lives together as a result of our trials and tribulations over the years. We renew our plan to continue with our daily celebration of our married life, rather than just on one specific day in a year.

Perhaps, we are still in the Go Go state of retirement, but I think we may be fast approaching some form of the Go Slow state and that will be okay too when it arrives. Together we will just turn another page in our journey of life, and continue on our way.

The End

BIBLIOGRAPHY

My heartfelt thanks to the authors and publishers for permission to quote the following:

From Thomas Moore, *Soul Mates*: HarperCollins Publisher, 1994

From Harold Kushner, *How Good Do We Have To Be*: First Avon Books, 1983

From *The Measure of Our Success* by Marian Wright Edelman. Copyright 1992 by Marian Wright Edelman: Reprinted by permission of Beacon Press, Boston

ABOUT THE AUTHOR

I grew up in a very small town in western New York state on a forty-eight-acre farm with work horses, cows, chickens, pigs, and dogs. Shortly after obtaining my high school diploma in 1955 I found a job and moved to Rochester, where I attended night school at the University of Rochester.

I found the girl of my dreams, Katie, in 1960 and we married a year later. We have two children, John and Katherine. My working career covered forty-one years in finance with three different employers, before retiring in 1996 at the age of fifty-seven from SunTrust Bank in Tampa, Florida.

My wife and I sailed our Columbia 8.7 until 2003 ending thirty-five years of joyful sailing. We continue to pursue our dreams and enjoy our life together, sharing and walking on the white sand beaches in Florida, and traveling to distant places.

— George J. Zeller

Clearwater, FL 2009